7780 1677

OVERSTATED

OVERSTATED

A COAST-TO-COAST ROAST OF THE 50 STATES

★ ★ ★

COLIN QUINN

ST. MARTIN'S
PRESS
NEW YORK

First published in the United States by St. Martin's Press,
an imprint of St. Martin's Publishing Group

OVERSTATED. Copyright © 2020 by Colin Quinn. All rights reserved. Printed in the
United States of America. For information, address St. Martin's Publishing Group,
120 Broadway, New York, NY 10271.

www.stmartins.com

Designed by Steven Seighman

The Library of Congress Cataloging-in-Publication Data is available upon request.

ISBN 978-1-250-26844-0 (hardcover)
ISBN 978-1-250-26845-7 (ebook)

Our books may be purchased in bulk for promotional, educational, or business
use. Please contact your local bookseller or the Macmillan Corporate and
Premium Sales Department at 1-800-221-7945, extension 5442, or by email at
MacmillanSpecialMarkets@macmillan.com.

First Edition: 2020

10 9 8 7 6 5 4 3 2 1

To CQ. I realize it might come off as conceited and selfish to some to dedicate a book to myself, but I couldn't think of anyone more deserving. And I hope the American people will realize what I've meant to this country.

Nothing is more wonderful than the art of being free but nothing is harder to learn than how to use freedom.

—TOCQUEVILLE

CONTENTS

THE SOUTHWEST

THE WEST

THE PACIFIC COAST

THE COUNTRY'S FOSTER CHILDREN

THE AMERICAN ROME

INVENTORY OR AUTOPSY

INTRODUCTION

I've been to 47 of the 50 states, not counting the Dakotas and Wyoming, so I guess I've been to all 50. And I'd always be excited to visit the different states over the years after reading and seeing about them on TV.

But every time I go to different states it's like going to a family wedding or reunion where all the distant cousins are gathered. You get that feeling that these people are nothing like you. You can't believe you are related to them. But then you see them make a gesture or a facial expression and you go, "Oh yeah, I see how we have the same blood." Like when two Americans that don't know each other are in another country at the same hotel, we will look over at each other like "Do you believe they put up with this?" Because one thing about all Americans, for better or for worse, we don't like to put up with any bureaucratic abuse or any authority dismissing us. Whether you are from New York City, like I am, or some small town, you are used to people having to deal with you as a citizen. We took the concept of "the citizen" and weaponized it. Before that you were a serf or a merchant or a soldier. And if you stood in front of any person or institution that represented the king and complained, they would either laugh you off or kill you. That's day 1 of being American. "I know my rights! You aren't better than me."

But now everybody has taken it to the place where individual rights are just used by annoying people. To criticizing everything, to breaking off into factions just like James Madison was worried would happen. And the loudest and most extreme will always be heard. Because when people no longer believe in representative democracy, the next step has to be mob rule. Now we are in the factions moment in history, where everybody is broken up into cults trying to force their values and ideals onto each other, and so far, it's not looking very promising for our future. Because everybody has known since Cain and Abel that blood relatives shouldn't fight. That's something the Kardashians know that nobody else seems to realize. So here is the story of America. It's not always pretty, but it's not always ugly. It's got ego and pride and good deeds and sacrifice and selfishness and honor and greed. It's a triumph and a tragedy and it's a miraculous success and a noble failure. A toast to us! The Americans: the most self-centered, enthusiastic, discontented spiritual materialists in history. The world will never see the likes of us again. It's like your life and my life on a bigger scale (and not boring).

So, 244 years later, here we are in 50-states couples' counseling and we are about to file papers for divorce. But before we do that we have to ask: Is this what we really want? It's a big decision, so we should look at what we did and how amazing it was and how impossible it was and then if we still say break up, we break up. It's been done before.

You have to go back to the beginning. At the beginning of the sixteenth century you had the big four: England, France, Spain, and Portugal. Nobody else really had international clout. If any of the big four noticed you, you had to become their colony. And the only choice you had was who you would let be your colonial master. So South America up to Georgia and Louisiana was Spain and Portugal, France was everything west of Newark and everything north of the Berkshires (or the lyrics to the first two James Taylor albums), and England was everything from

Boston Harbor through Virginia, North Carolina, and the rest of the secondhand Smoky Mountains. The American colonies eventually negotiated, maneuvered, or outfought all the big-four historical empires out of all of it, and the only reason we stopped was because we had nowhere to go except to drown in the Pacific. Along the way, as we all know, it wasn't the most ethical or bloodless journey. But it was ours, good and bad.

NEW ENGLAND

*The New England conscience doesn't keep you from doing
what you shouldn't, it just keeps you from enjoying it.*
—Isaac Bashevis Singer

Plymouth Rock was all about the religious people. They had slavery, but much less of it than in other places because they didn't need it for their economy. And by 1790 it was outlawed. On the other hand, Jamestown was all about the businesspeople. Slavery, money. Not equality. Individualism. You had a paradox already, right from the start. Nothing less than an odd couple when you think about it. People that were all about spirituality and people that were all about the material. These two types teamed up to make the thirteen colonies, because when you have a common enemy—England—that tends to bind you. And they both had immigrants whom they could send out to live their dream of the New World. The religious and the business types both sent their representatives to "claim" the land and push out the Brits, French, and Spaniards, so even though they thought differently, the two types of original colonists had the same strategy. The big difference was that the North was all about not being like England, no matter what. And the South was about being better than England by using England's own earlier economic system—the essential feudal system of classes—to succeed and undercut them. It's like the two sons that both hate their father, but one becomes the opposite of their father and the other becomes just like him.

★ ★ ★

CONNECTICUT

RICH MAN, POOR MAN

Connecticut and Massachusetts and Virginia are really the beginning of the country. Without them, what do you have? You would've started with Delaware and Rhode Island—and no offense but . . . Connecticut was much more important than it is now, because of the Fundamental Orders of Connecticut, which was actually the inspiration for the U.S. Constitution. So that's pretty impressive. I mean, it's on their license plate, so that means they are proud of it. Not that anybody cares. Connecticut probably hopes somebody will ask: "Why does it say CONSTITUTION STATE on your license plate?" But nobody does. And they've got to be proud too of the famous constitutional decision known as the Connecticut Compromise. Because Roger Sherman went home for a weekend break when none of the founding fathers could decide whether we should have direct democracy and came up with the two senators per state vs. Congress vs. Electoral College arrangement. That's the infamous part of the Constitution that got Trump elected. So, stop blaming the red states for Trump, put the responsibility where it belongs, Connecticut.

Connecticut is also the state that Tocqueville first talked about as formative for creating an American personality. He talked about how its citizens (and Americans in general) were religious but still civic-minded and materialistic. He describes how residents of Connecticut and all of New England were obsessed with local politics and how we set up these townships where everybody switched jobs to become part of the select committee or the magistrate or the council. And this was before the Constitution. People were already obsessed with free speech. That's what people came here for: conversation. And that's what the founding fathers delivered in the Bill of Rights. Those early days in Connecticut are why.

Connecticut is also a cushion between Massachusetts and New York. A high-end cushion but still a cushion. That's why they have no pro football, baseball, or basketball teams, because they agreed the lower half of the state would be for the Yankees and the upper half for the Boston Red Sox. That rivalry was so intense that they had to put a state in between the residents just to keep it from starting a war. It's like the 38th parallel for states. Connecticut's a state that carries a lot of symbolism. It's got the image of being the rich state. And we love that, because you always want to have somebody that looks like they are enjoying their life in a way you never could. You would rather it was you, but at least somebody's living it up. I give the rich people in Connecticut credit. They know how to do it. I was in Old Saybrook and they don't even have a KFC or a Papa John's. You eat on a back porch and they have a cello and a violist and there's a rich old lady who goes there alone every day since her husband died in 1998 and she orders the same thing every evening, probably a Waldorf salad and a whiskey sour. Connecticut's got a lot of one-percenters—and I don't mean the outlaw-biker kind. Isn't it weird that somehow the outlaw biker one-percenter is now the ultrarich? There's not really a lot of crossover since Malcolm Forbes died. But that's Connecticut. They are very rich and very poor. They can't make up their mind. Is it the hood or the yacht club? Bridgeport, Hartford, New Haven, Waterbury—I could go on—these are all serious gang cities. Then you have the topsiders. New

Canaan, Darien, and Greenwich Yacht Clubs and Dockers and tennis or polo or whatever clichés you think of when you think of WASPs. Then you've got cities that are basically at war. Hartford was the insurance capital of the world, yet the one place that you can't get insurance right now is Hartford. People moved because they knew it was a death trap. I spent three weeks in gun-wavin' New Haven a few summers ago doing my show and the city is Yale kids running for their student housing once the sun goes down. When class lets out, it's like watching a herd of wildebeests trying to make it past a pride of lions. That's Connecticut. It's the extremes of America all rolled into one. The haves, the have-nots, and then all the middle people. There's a lot of blue-collar towns in Connecticut, but nobody cares about them because people like to have certain images and we all love the idea of the lock-jawed Connecticut tennis couple with the white cable-knit sweaters around their shoulders It makes you feel good to know that they can exist. And at the same time, you feel better than them in some way because they are sheltered and snobby and clueless and you are down-to-earth and cool.

So, Connecticut is a state that was important and it still matters not because of what it is but because of what it represents. Because in a country that prides itself on getting rid of the class system, we still want to know that somebody is rich. Even if you want to kill them or take them down or Bernie Sanders them financially, you still want them to exist. So, Connecticut set the tone in a lot of ways. It's the relative that pisses you off to visit because they make you feel like you're not doing it right, but at the same time they always have crab and shrimp platters at their parties and they have a nice lawn and they are gracious. And that's what I think America was and is for a lot of people from other countries. It is the Connecticut of countries. A place you have that love/hate relationship with. I guarantee even ISIS talks about America as the great Satan but then one of them says, "I heard one of those filthy decadent infidel Western restaurants has unlimited breadsticks." And then they all feel a shiver of excitement over the concept of unrestricted amounts of food.

MASSACHUSETTS

TAX THIS, KID

Massachusetts. Every house is a colonial. There are historical plaques all over the place honoring guys named Ezekiel and Zachary. To be fair, they are where it all started in Plymouth Rock, so you have to give them credit. And they were really into the political process. Town halls and councils and sit-downs and committees. Tocqueville said it. He said the average Massachusetts person's love of discourse brought to mind ancient Athens. I'm sure he wouldn't feel that way if he were in the bleachers in Fenway listening to a couple of cock-knockers from Everett cursing and whipping Cracker Jacks at a group of kids wearing Tufts sweatshirts. Massachusetts has gotten very cocky from the Revere/Adams era to the Belichick/Brady era. Used to be the pride of Massachusetts were all those charming colonial-era towns like Lexington and Concord and the House of Seven Gables—now it's getting the finger on I-90 by a fat landscaper in a scally cap and a Dropkick Murphys hoodie.

Last time I was in Plymouth, we did a comedy show at The Memorial Hall, and afterward there was a huge brawl outside in the snow. And this young girl ran up to us, and I thought she was scared and I felt bad that she had to witness bloodshed and violence in this beautiful snow-covered historic town square. Until she looked at us and said, "Great fight!" and smiled like she had been asked for her hand in marriage in a Jane Austen novel. But that's how Massachusetts does it. Even Boston Harbor. They didn't have to throw the tea in the water. They could've just stolen it. But they wanted to start a fight.

These states are important. Massachusetts and Connecticut are where our system got invented. Believe me, I don't like to admit it either. But a lot of the early ideas and "habits" that became our system started here. Puritans take a lot of abuse for being tight-asses and religious and a lot of the other qualities that are considered negatives in contemporary society. But you have to give them credit. They wanted to not be England so badly that they came up with some great ideas for "systemic change." And freedom of religion was an important ingredient. Because as flawed as religions are, they do speak to one eternal truth: which is people are always going to have to try to corral their baser instincts. And if you don't call it out, then it seems like it's okay. Because humanity will always be humanity. Even though we may advance technologically, human nature stays the same. We get sidetracked by our character faults. We live the seven deadly sins every bit as much as they did in colonial times, only now they are digital:

Facebook is envy.

Twitter is wrath.

Instagram is pride, lust, gluttony, greed, and sloth.

The internet is original sin. It's all the knowledge in the world. The tree of knowledge. And now we have it. But in Genesis humans aren't supposed to have all that access to information, because we can't handle it. And yet we ate the apple and got all the knowledge and the first thing we saw is each other naked. And what's the first thing we did when the internet came out? Looked at each other naked. And what's the name of the biggest computer company? Apple. And Steve Jobs said he named it after apple orchards because he thought it sounded cheerful. I know what he was thinking subconsciously. Plus, Steve Jobs was known to be an occasionally satanic guy. Wouldn't it be just like the devil to get us to eat the forbidden fruit again all these years later? The point is that a little religion is a nice balance against the material world, and the early arrivals knew it. Freedom of speech was another of our early national ideals, but the problem with it, is that no one ever changes their opinion. Historically, the only time anyone changes their opinion is right after they lose a war. Standing there in rags and rubble with dead bodies surrounding you and then you start to think, "They may have a point. Next time they speak to me, I'm going to listen a little more closely." And the problem with the Puritans was they were human, and humans are willful. They wanted people to follow the path of what they believed was the best way to think and behave. So whether your belief is God or discourse, some other members of humanity who believe the other thing will find a way to wreck it.

There are Puritan descendants embedded all over our DNA. They were the fundamentalists and then the moral majority and then the Christian Coalition and now they are the social justice warriors (SJWs). From the stopping of speakers to getting rid of books to controlling offensive and blasphemous language—these were all the province of the Christian right for many years. Starting with the Puritans. Ironically, the Puritan doctrine became the doctrine of the SJWs. That group has picked up the same techniques the Puritans used: banning, shunning, and all for the greater good.

I take it personally because I take everything personally—but also, because I'm a comedian, I see the way these new Puritan SJWs are monitoring comedy. Stand-up comedy. That dangerous mouthpiece of tyranny. That murderous apparatus of the fascists. The Nazis were well known for their flourishing stand-up comedy scene. Just the fact that people are trying to enforce standards that are "acceptable" in stand-up comedy tells me they are not coming from the place they claim to be coming from. And this worldview is under the unquestioned idea that there is punching up and punching down in comedy. I have an alternative description of comedy. It's not punching! People don't tend to leave comedy clubs frothing at the mouth to start committing hate crimes. Comedy isn't punching. It's verbal sparring. It's play fighting!! Why is no one concerned about this movement to remove comedy unless it's committee-approved by six people who have never smiled or laughed but sure are woke? Comedy doesn't work best when people are standing next to you asking you to justify your language, clarify your meaning, and articulate your intentions and beliefs. That's good to find out about someone if they're a Supreme Court nominee. Just admit you are the new *Footloose* parents. But the SJWs don't admit that; I'm sure they feel just the way the Puritans felt as they tied somebody down for a quick dunk out in Provincetown.

Either you see this country as a predatory, unfair, crooked, biased, amoral abyss. Or you see it as a pure, unsullied, generous, virtuous, blameless paradise. Why can't it be both? Because there's no room for incongruity and contradiction in how we see things. People like good and bad. No wavering. Belief. Conviction. Dogmatism. Staunch definitive. No doubt, and these are where factions take over. And now we have social media, where you literally can't be interrupted as you give your opinion like it's gospel. Like the Pilgrims. So maybe we took that civic-minded early Puritan ideal of a society and turned it into a bunch of Monday-morning quarterbacks and that's not a Colin Kaepernick joke. Maybe some people feel we should've just turned around and gone back to England and Holland. But either way, America is where it ended up happening and, say what you want, we blew the world's mind for a few hundred years. And it all started on a stupid little landing strip on Plymouth Bay with the first "settlers."

I place "settlers" in quotations because there's a lot of terminology that has been viewed through the lens of the people who suffered under the pilgrimage. Or expedition. Or invasion. Calling it a discovery is inaccurate: the term "New World" must've been chilling to hear for the people living in what they considered to be the present world. We can sit here and curse ourselves and beg forgiveness or seek penance, but it happened the way it happened and nothing is going to change that. Give up all hope of having a better past. So at this point we all know that for some people "Plymouth Rock landed on them." And it's also the fact that for a long time our history chose to show only the bright side and to act like none of the bad ever happened. It's one of the positive qualities of America—our enthusiasm and the sunny-side-up attitude. But the dark side is that many people didn't benefit, and if you're among them, you don't want to hear that rah-rah-rah talk. But now we've done a complete 180, where we actually only speak negatively of the United States and the founding fathers and the white Europeans, which is also not a full story either.

There are a lot of contradictory things in our makeup starting with the slave-owning founding fathers who also set the world free. That's the American way. We take everything and instead of nuance and gray areas, we see either the greatest thing or the worst thing. Sometimes I look at the ideals of this country and feel disappointed. Because we thought we'd be different. We all swore we wouldn't spend our whole lives arguing, bickering, and laughing at dumb shit. But we do. We used up our freedom of assembly to line up for new Yeezys. We used our free speech to curse out umpires and refs. Technology to jerk off to. We used our literacy to read comment sections. Do you know how many books Tolstoy sold last year? Probably three. Meanwhile there's a You-Tube video of a wedding party falling off a dock that got seven million views. Another couple of billion for a fish playing cards with a goat. When you set up a country and say free buffet, you can't complain when everybody ignores the steamed vegetables.

NEW HAMPSHIRE

THE SLOGAN DON DRAPER WISHES HE'D COME UP WITH

Live Free or Die. It was adopted from a toast by General John Stark, shooting guard for the Knicks and hero of the Revolutionary War. Even though Patrick Henry said, Give Me Liberty or Give Me Death, which is basically the same thing, twenty years before that. But people are forgotten, while license plates live forever. And Give Me Liberty or Give Me Death doesn't fit on a license plate. As they say, brevity is the soul of the Department of Motor Vehicles. New Hampshire was the first state to declare its independence from Britain. The big difference between states in New England and the rest of the states is that, unlike the rest of the country, in New England they don't like to make small talk. No "Hello," no "How's your day going?" Just grunts and severe looks. I don't know if it's Puritan blood or the cold or the proximity to Maine. New Hampshire got a visit from Paul Revere way before his midnight ride, and even he wasn't a big talker. "The British are coming!" That's all he said. He didn't say, "Hey, everybody, I heard something tonight that I think you should hear. It's a rumor, but it's from a reliable source." No. He just said his four words and that was it. But first he went up to Portsmouth to tell them the British were going to take over the fort. Four hundred people went up there and raided the place and lowered the British flag. Which was a pretty radical move in those days, when you think about it. Nobody fucked with the British flag. It was the height of the British Empire. It would be like going into a rough sports bar and turning off the game everyone's watching and putting on *The Devil Wears Prada*. You're asking for it. So that's why New Hampshire has the audacity to say Live Free or Die. Then you have the other side of the coin. Bretton Woods Royal Economic Forum (basically a junior college Bilderberg). Pretty shady move to meet in the woods of New Hampshire to discuss our finances. It's also kind of sad that they had this big financial event in New Hampshire, which is known for its fierce commitment to liberty. Live Free or Do a Leveraged Buyout.

They are the big state for the campaign caucuses. Them and Iowa. They're both small states. They represent the country the way it sees itself. Humble, mom-and-pop. Maybe a town square. A town hall. A library. Old-school Americana. Once every four years people in New Hampshire get to live it up. Have the media stop by. Rent out the bed-and-breakfasts. All the local dirtbags become Uber drivers. The local paper gets to interview some of their idols because they have them trapped at the diner. They are a couple of quiet states that just made one assertive move in their lives. They said, "We will be the early registered states to pick the candidates for president." And they have a couple of months of excitement. New York or Texas or California couldn't do it. It'd be overkill. People just robbing and stealing and everything else. They'd just smell money and it'd be a feeding frenzy. States like Iowa and New Hampshire are old-school: they like money, but they don't go into a frenzy. I'm sure it's not all the hookers and the drug dealers and the business wheeler-dealers invading the local hotel bars trying to find a way to separate everybody and get their money or their influence. It's civilized. I've been to New Hampshire and it's civilized as much as any place can be, I guess. And Live Free or Die is maybe one of the most famous slogans ever. And in a country where advertising came into being, that's enough.

RHODE ISLAND

FOUNDING FATHERS TO GODFATHERS

Roger Williams is the guy who started Rhode Island. He was a Puritan minister. The Puritans believed in "work, church, and home," as they say. No time for lollygagging, as Joe Biden might put it. No drinking, no joking around. The other thing with the Rhode Island Puritans was that there was no sex involved. That kind of throws a person into a new way of looking at life. Nobody mentions sex in any document in the first hundred years of the United States. Because the Puritans understood that there was no way to build a functional society with sex involved. When you are growing crops and building barns and forming political systems, there's no time to be jerking off, literally or figuratively. If the early settlers had access to today's pornography and the random sexual promiscuity that we have enjoyed, they would all be living in shacks on the shores of Narragansett like a bunch of stoners. They'd spend all day bodysurfing in those cloaks and stockings and at night they'd change into bikinis and board shorts and sit around campfires, roasting marshmallows and dancing along to Sublime and Sugar Ray like it's the summer of '98. If you wanted to escape from the other colonies, you could come up and see Roger Williams. He made the state with a code, where you keep your mouth shut about who's coming in and who's going out. Everybody would pretend they didn't see the people heading in either direction. It was another of those unwritten rules. If people come up here asking questions, you don't tell them anything. You don't know anything. And that's why Rhode Island became a mafia state. Because the tradition was to keep your mouth shut about who's there and what's going on up there. They were the state that refused to ratify the Constitution. Everybody else was on board except them. That's because they had a paper money of their own and they thought they would take a beating financially if they joined. Even then they had some kind of money-laundering scheme going on up there. Rhode Island is run by Mafia and old money. Really old money. They look down on Connecticut like it's Rodney Dangerfield in *Caddyshack*.

They've got the *Mayflower* descendants living next door to the guys who fell off a truck from Naples. You've got tracksuits vs. Dockers—people who wear ascots around their necks or gold chains, college or pinky rings. The first time I did comedy in Providence back in the 80s at a club called Periwinkles in the mall, I was up there bombing away and then suddenly I started doing this very linguistically specific stuff about Italians in Brooklyn and the crowd started to go nuts and it saved my set. Like many people, I had a very parochial view of life, seeing Italians as being only from New York and New Jersey and maybe Philadelphia, but that show taught me that every ethnicity has certain commonalities that transcend where the actual people landed. But of course, saying that today is troublesome. So let's just say that what that show taught me was that when you use easy stereotypes against a historically marginalized group, it's playing into tropes that are outdated and tone deaf.

Then Rhode Island has Newport, which was the first rich people's vacation place. And where Bob Dylan scandalized the folk world by playing an electric guitar. It seems silly now that people booed him, but it's kind of cool that anybody could get that worked up about something artistic. Especially folk fans, who are not exactly known for their violent outbursts. To them it must have been what it would be like for comedy fans to see Dave Attell suddenly come out on stage smashing watermelons.

The only unplanned nuclear explosion in America was in 1964 in Charlestown, Rhode Island, when a worker put too much uranium solution in a tank and it exploded. He was the only casualty. It makes me less scared of nuclear accidents to discover they basically have the same mortality rate as a brick falling off a roof. And it was his fault. It's like the asshole that lit the cigarette that burned down Notre Dame. One dummy destroyed one of the last wonders of the world. Makes you think maybe that's what happened to the other wonders. Hanging Gardens of Babylon: some idiot probably left his wine sack and then he comes back after the weekend and there were ten thousand fruit flies that had reduced the gardens to four-square feet of crab grass. Who knows? And with the organized crime in Rhode Island, I'm suspicious that nuclear "accident" might've been nuclear "on purpose."

That's the way things go. Everybody thinks they are doing one thing when they are really doing the opposite. And the United States was not immune. So, when the Puritans were coming over, they didn't think, "Hey, we are going to take over and open the door for a lot of dirtbags." They thought, "We have to get away from these assholes in our country and here's our opportunity. Just like when you moved away from your house or city or state. You went with the intention of living your best life. That's what the Puritans were doing. They didn't realize they were opening the door to a lot of stragglers. When you moved, you didn't know your drug addict cousins were going to follow you and ruin everything and use your good name to get people to trust them. Well, that's the history of America. It was decent people trying to escape their past and not realizing you can never escape your past; it follows you and ruins your credit rating. Rhode Island started with Roger Williams, a man who created a place that was the first place to separate church and state and ended up with leaders who separated church and state like the baptism scene in *The Godfather*.

★ ★ ★

VERMONT

THE OLD HIPPIE

Vermont is the friendliest of the New England states, which is not that hard to be but still. They've always been beautiful but they don't show off. They dress down. They underplay it. Not a lot of makeup. In fact, it's illegal to sell makeup in New England in general. I think you can sell blush in Connecticut and eye makeup in Rhode Island. But that's about it.

Vermont was its own country until 1791. Had its own currency and everything. The coins didn't have pictures of the president—they had a bearded guy in a parka vest with a Neutral Milk Hotel T-shirt. Every guy in Vermont has a beard. I know everybody in America has a beard now, but in Vermont they've been like that forever. They were hippies right away. Nobody knows why Vermont has more hippies than any other state. Maybe just when everybody got back to nature in the early 70s, the New York–area hippies said, "We will go to Vermont." The West Coast went to Northern California (because of the weed), the Southwest hippies went to Austin, the Southeast hippies went to Asheville, and the Midwestern ones maybe Yellow Springs, Ohio? The other problem is the old people have too much energy from eating organic so you have relevant old people like Bernie Sanders and Ben and Jerry. There's no other place where the old people are the most famous and relevant residents. So people go up there to visit. Skiers, of course. But also, to check out the foliage. Watch the leaves turn color. It's a pretty good tourism idea. We could do that in New York—we *should* do that. Watch the snow turn into carbon dioxide–coated slush in two hours.

Over 500,000 gallons of maple syrup a year make Vermont the largest producer in the United States. That must be the hardest job. Trying to transfer that sticky shit into bottles without getting it all over your clothes. I bet people up there hate the smell of maple syrup because it reminds them of work. Even worse, factory work. It's like in China—you show them an iPhone, they get traumatized and start screaming their brains out.

It's not just maple syrup. Vermont is also the number one producer of marble. Although marble is not as popular as it used to be. When billionaires wanted everybody to know how rich they were, it was a booming business. Half their houses were marble. The best time to make marble was Roman Empire. Everything was a marble pillar to them. They were crazy about them. Now nobody uses marble pillars except international arms dealers, and how many of them are you going to run into when you spend half your days at the craft store in Montpelier? Vermont is the least religious state at only 22 percent, which is still pretty high. Of the people I know who go to church regularly, I'd say it's closer to minus 22 percent in most places.

They also gave women rights in 1880, when women's rights consisted of having the right to go to the stove and then go beat clothes on a rock. In those days a woman would say, "My husband knows I get to decide what time dinner gets put on that table, and I don't want no backtalk!" And the other women would say, "Oh, Gertie, you are a real feminist, I do declare." The Green Mountain boys were the militia. First named to fight against a land war with New York but then reformed for the

American Revolution and the Civil War, they will still fight if they have to, I'm sure, but will quote Noam Chomsky the entire time. They would probably surround the enemy and say, "Come out with your hands up. We are here to reinforce the ruling class and to manufacture consent!" Then they throw in a Molotov cocktail filled with patchouli oil.

The band Phish is from Vermont, which shocks no one. If the band Phish can't be from Vermont, then what's it all mean? Also, the recipient of the first Social Security check in 1940 was a Vermonter and she lived to be 100—so I guess she really gambled on the system and won. But it's not her fault. I'm sure there's somebody else that retired and dropped dead the next day. Montpelier is the only state capital with no McDonald's. They had a McDonald's in Burlington but it went out of business. That's pretty powerful. Especially since it has the largest cow-to-people ratio in the nation. Maybe those cows put out that energy like, "Hey, it's pretty disrespectful considering we are the majority here. Come on, how would you people like it if we put up a cemetery in the middle of town? That's what it is for us." And they didn't have a Walmart till the 90s. That's what makes the country so wild. Vermont is gonna be Vermont. And nobody tells them you can't be who you want to be. Because people in Vermont don't do things the way people in Kansas do. But we still want the other states to change. And be more like us. And the only reason we never broke up was because we all lived with the marriage lie. "They'll change. Give it time. They will come around." And nobody came around. And now every little thing we do annoys each other.

And social media was like a couple arguing, and even though we argued, we lived in separate parts of the house, but now with constant electronic connectivity, we work from home and are around each other day and night.

And that's where we are at. Trying to legally and culturally accommodate a country that has a Vermont and a Kansas living by the same rules. It's pretty amazing that we pulled it off for as long as we did, really.

MAINE

THE NEW ENGLAND OF NEW ENGLAND

They are strange and quiet—not nice, but clean. They give us the creeps but that's their thing. The reason that Maine is at the top of the East Coast of the country is because it was the way America was at the beginning. It's like the Midwest of the East. Mainers are quiet. They understand that life isn't about words. I used to think: "Those idiots up there. You can't hold a conversation with them." But now I see it's not that. It's because they know conversation is 90 percent bullshit. First of all, they get up at four in the morning, because it's a lobster culture. So even if you aren't setting traps, your body knows that something is going on and it wakes you up. And that's one of the main reasons they are quiet: they don't want to wake up anybody who's sleeping in. (Sleeping in up there means 5:15 A.M.) But the point is that there are about ten states where they get up early, and Maine is the earliest of the early risers. When you are in charge of 90 percent of the country's lobster, it gives you a sense of responsibility to all shellfish lovers. Because, let's face it, when you go to have shellfish it's usually shrimp or crabs or something else, but if there's no lobster there you feel like something's off. Maine used to be very poor. Because lobster was only eaten by four people: Rockefeller, Astor, J. P. Morgan, and Andrew Carnegie. Nobody else could afford lobster. In the old days, lobster was a delicacy only for the rich. Then I don't know what happened, but suddenly people in Maine worked eight-hour shifts instead of sitting home waiting to hear from one of Rockefeller's butlers. "Excuse me, but Mr. Rockefeller is in the mood for a three-pounder this evening, if you would be so kind" type of thing.

Otherwise, there's not too much to say about Maine. That's what happens when you don't talk much: people don't talk much about you. The squeaky wheel gets the grease. You don't want publicity. Even Stephen King doesn't really make a big deal out of himself. He's sold 350 million books and he still hangs out in the local diner. It's got that one senator, Susan Collins, who epitomizes Maine because she pisses off the left and the right. She votes yes when you think she's gonna vote no and she votes no when you think she's gonna vote yes. I admire that. But that's how they say people in Maine are. Very oppositional for no reason. If they think you want them to do something, they've got to do the opposite.

Maine was part of the Commonwealth of Massachusetts until 1820, when they voted to secede. And I'm sure Massachusetts felt like a big weight had been lifted off its chest. Maine looms up there, both physically and psychologically. Looking down at the rest of New England like everybody else is frivolous and soft. They are the Spartans of New England. They are the New England of the rest of New England. There's always one state like that. The one that makes the other states in their region feel like that region makes everybody else in the country feel. Like Mississippi makes Alabama and Tennessee feel like a bunch of Yankee city slickers. Or how Nebraska makes Kansas and Iowa feel like a bunch of lazy urbanites. That's one of the things about being such a large country. Instead of having culture clashes with other countries, you just have them with yourself.

People in Maine also have felt like outsiders since the beginning. They were the border against the French in Canada. So, while the rest of us were fighting England, they were fighting England and France. They've always been the quiet state. They don't cause a lot of trouble. I don't think they can vote in national elections, although I could be wrong on that one. They are solid and dependable. Being a border state is a big responsibility. Border states don't get enough credit. It's like being a doorman at a nightclub. You don't decide who gets in or who doesn't, but you have to make sure to control the crowd. Now, it's true being a border state in the North is a lot different than being one in the South. Canada and Mexico are polar opposites. Not literally "polar" opposites, but you know what I mean. Mexicans are trying to come in and Canadians aren't trying to come in. The only Canadians I know that like it here are Norm Macdonald, Bonnie McFarlane, and Phil Hanley, and they all could easily be from Maine, personalities-wise. (If you don't know Phil Hanley, he's a comedian who's famous for giving me the title of this book.) They are all thin and taciturn and cynical. That's another thing about Maine people. They have a really biting way of speaking. They don't say much, but when they speak it's usually very hurtful and sarcastic. But that's how a border state should be. Very stern and letting people know, "Hey, this is America. Don't fuck around here. We don't like people getting crazy in here." That's why a place like Washington State isn't a good border state. Because Washington never judges anybody. If there's no judgment, then people don't know what the rules are. Hell, I've lived here my whole life and I don't know what the rules are.

Maine is the conscience of New England and it keeps the rest of the states from getting too full of themselves.

In these days, when coronavirus is destroying us, it's important to remember that, ironically, America would not have triumphed if we didn't have our greatest ally, which was disease.

PATRIOTIC DISEASES

SMALLPOX

The perfect disease to conquer a nation. It killed half the Native Americans when Europeans first arrived. The explorers are going, "This is manifest destiny, what's the thread count on the last of the Mohicans?"

YELLOW FEVER

It won real estate salesman of the year in 1803. It killed the French troops in Haiti, which caused France to lose Haiti and caused Napoleon to spiral into a depression/existential crisis, leading him to sell us half of what is now the country for $15 million. Bargain-basement rates. So, we owe our country to a bunch of mosquitos that didn't wash their hands.

CHOLERA

Was a big one for settling the country. They said the Irish immigrants brought it over, and I can tell you that's a vicious lie and I don't need evidence. It made a lot of people travel west because the cities were incubators for this kind of thing. It killed former President Polk and then made its way across the country to the California, Oregon, and Mormon trails. Spread down the Mississippi.

Cholera was always fatal. In those days, you got cholera and people would say, "Hey, man, we had some laughs together, huh? Can I have your boots?" Because they knew the treatment (morphine, opium, and draining your blood through the veins in your arm) was going to finish whatever cholera started.

MEASLES

Soldier killer of the Civil War. Two-thirds of the Civil War soldiers' deaths were from disease. So when people do those Civil War battlefield reenactments, they should have 70 percent of those soldiers just coughing in the trenches.

SHAME DISEASES

SYPHILIS

Nobody wanted to die of that one because people would laugh at your funeral. But it was one of the top killers in this country for a hundred years.

SCARLET FEVER

That was a girl's disease, as you can tell by the name. No guy wanted to die of scarlet fever. Again, they would laugh at your funeral.

STUPIDLY NAMED DISEASES

DROPSY

Swells up your body. Fluid retention. Heart failure. They used to throw some leeches on there and let them drain it out. Leeches were the early surgeons. The family would wait for the leech to come off the body and the leech would wipe his brow and say, "I'm sorry. We did all we could."

SCURVY

It only affected sailors. They would give you a lime to cure it. That's why the British were called "limeys," which is considered a derogatory term. It's the most positive ethnic insult there is. "Ahoy, you citrus fruit that destroys bacterial infection." "Whoa, watch it with the hate speech."

TYPHOID

Killed President Harrison thirty days in, which led to the vice president John Tyler being allowed to take over, which led to the 25th Amendment. And we all know what that means.

CONSUMPTION

You'd be sent right to a sanatorium. They had sanatoriums back then for anybody rich who had a disease and needed to quarantine. They were combination insane asylums, rehab joints, and spas. You could have three people in a natural spring and one is coughing up blood, the other is passed out on opium, and the third is J. P. Morgan's loser nephew.

THE PATHOGENS TO POWER

Coronavirus is gonna bring us back to post-Revolutionary War America. There was no physical contact. A nod of the head was the bro hug. In the old days, a son would go off to war; the father would nod his head good-bye, and they both knew it meant "I love you." A daughter would get married; the father would be reading the paper and smoking a pipe. He wouldn't even get up from his chair. He would just look at her fiancé and say, "You take care of my little girl." People self-quarantined all the time. Because there were only books for entertainment. Watching TV is fun to do with other people. Reading books is a solitary activity. There were no large gatherings. If more than ten people got together, it meant there was about to be a war. People didn't assemble because they were too busy to assemble. They thought a gathering was indulgent because that meant you weren't chopping or digging or planting. People would say, "What are you up to lately?" And you couldn't say, "I'm thinking about life." You would have to say, "I'm painting a fence. I'm framing a barn. I'm sewing a coat." Everything had to be made from scratch. The good thing about this virus is that it showed us the thin veneer of civilization. People then were always on the verge of anarchy. They were always a few days away from starvation. Everybody knew people who had starved to death. People starving is a very frightening thing. And it makes you mean. People fight in stores over nonessentials like toilet paper. Can you imagine what would happen if you couldn't eat for a week? I get irritable if I'm at the diner and my food takes too long. That's 15 minutes. In one day, 24 hours would be 15 minutes 96 times. That makes you 96 times angrier than at that moment. That level of anger could easily bite the head off a bird. Now in 4 days, that's almost 400 times that anger on top of the physical discomfort of the symptoms of starvation. Your mind wouldn't even be in charge. Your body would take over all executive function. Next thing you know, you come out of a blackout and you're surrounded by a bunch of people in coonskin caps or local tribal clothes and you are happily munching away at an elk's carcass. It's survival. We're going back to frontier law. That's how the old West was, six feet distance. Don't come any closer. If you came within six feet of people, you were going to get shot unless you spoke your piece. People would talk about the best way to store potatoes for a whole day. Every conversation was about preserving food and trying to keep water clean and the best way to dress wounds. It was food, disease, and injury. So if this coronavirus doesn't end, we may have to discover "Canada."

★ ★ ★

MID-ATLANTIC

*America's history is longer, larger, more various,
more beautiful and more terrible than anything anyone
has ever said about it.*
—JAMES BALDWIN

★★★
DELAWARE

THE OUTLET MALL OF STATES

You want to talk about the disturbing states? Look at Delaware. These poor bastards are one of the original thirteen and nobody wants to admit they are a state. It's not just because they are small. It's because they are suspicious. In Delaware, there's no tax on anything. Nobody is sure why. Whenever politicians talk to people about raising and lowering taxes, people in Delaware are going: we don't give a shit. There are more businesses incorporated in Delaware than there are people. Fifty percent of all publicly traded companies in the United States are incorporated in Delaware. Over a million businesses. Obviously, there's somebody making money somehow on that deal. Delaware knows how to keep a secret. They make the Grand Caymans look like the Better Business Bureau. You can live there anonymously. Call yourself an LLC and you don't have to even give your name. Which makes it an ideal place to launder money, whether from a drug cartel or to plunder a nation's finances. I would like to start a shell corporation and do some international wire transfers. This is a big industry. You can hide your money in Delaware and nobody asks questions. You do your thing, and we know how to keep our mouths shut.

But even if we stopped Delaware from doing all this, do you think it would stop? Do you think there aren't hundreds of places in the world that wouldn't love to take Delaware's place? So that's the problem. We are in a position where you have to just avert your eyes because it's going to happen no matter what you do. It's just like prostitution or drugs. Either you do it or somebody else will. It's like in *The Godfather* when they tell Don Corleone, "Hey, if we don't get into drugs, then the families that do will get powerful and we will be destroyed." And Delaware is basically the Turk in that movie. He's the guy that says, "I'll be the bad guy." Delaware is the guy that will get his hands dirty. It's basically Switzerland if George Thorogood and the Destroyers were the von Trapp family.

Delaware even has its own royal family, the du Ponts. There are 3,000 of them all across the state. They are the Saudi royals of Delaware. Even down to the inbreeding. If you cross one, you cross them all. That's one reason the people in Delaware are so quiet. They know that there's always a du Pont around the corner. Delaware was the first state to ratify as a state—I guess that's one of the reasons they are so cocky and think they can make their own rules. It's the thing with Louisiana and Rhode Island also. They have just decided they will be countries within states. They don't care about national laws, and people admire that. These are the states that give states' rights a bad name. But people love it because everybody loves to make money, and if your state finds a loophole to make you money, everybody is going there. You don't see corporations going, "That sounds like you are abusing the system. I think I will incorporate in a more ethical state!" No, people like Delaware because they are the cynical friend that tells you right out loud so everyone can hear, "Hey, I can get you an iPhone for a hundred dollars." And you say, "How?" And they say, "Don't ask." That's Delaware's motto: "Welcome to Delaware. Don't ask, because once you know, you might be subpoenaed." Delaware gives you plausible deniability.

★ ★ ★

PENNSYLVANIA

CRADLE OF MONDAY-MORNING QUARTERBACKS

Our entire country's personality/outlook/mission statement started in Philadelphia. They decided that all these brand-new and relatively untried ideas could work. The whole representative thing, the whole Electoral College, the whole Bill of Rights. We keep trying to figure out why our system goes wrong. What are we doing to abuse this system? Maybe the system sometimes stinks too. You ever think a setup you've been using for 240 years that probably worked well for about 70 years in spurts isn't that infallible? First off, I've never been a fan of the Bill of Rights. Or the first two amendments. You've got free speech, free assembly, free press. Those three have been free a long time and what have they accomplished? Nothing but big mouths and traffic jams. The Second Amendment has accomplished a bunch of kids jumping under their desks when a car backfires. Third Amendment: you won't let a soldier be quartered in your house. Thank you for your service, but sleep outside on the stoop. Fourth Amendment: probable cause. So, some kid has the shape of a shotgun under his T-shirt, you're supposed to think it's just a lumpy sweater. Fifth Amendment: witness against yourself.

What if nobody else was there? Sixth—right to confront witnesses—sure, nothing like having a face to face with the murderer you're trying to put away for the rest of his life. Seventh: suing people. Yeah, that worked out well, we didn't abuse that one. Eighth: excessive bail. Bail is only good for the accused but bad for all your loved ones because if they don't bail you out, you can hold it over their heads for the rest of their lives. Ninth: there's a lot of stuff we didn't get as far as fundamental rights. Oh, so the founding fathers were the friends that help you move out of your old place but leave while your furniture is still on the street in front of the new one. Tenth Amendment: states vs. federal when it comes to powers. Three-branch system. Legislative, judicial, and executive. Thanks for the time bomb.

Speaking of Time Bombs . . .

ELECTORAL COLLEGE

Rutherford B. Hayes won the election of 1876 because he agreed to stop Reconstruction. Samuel Tilden got screwed. He got backstabbed by both parties, even though he won the popular and the Electoral College vote. Here's why you know the Electoral College was not that great of an idea. Nobody copied us. Well, not nobody, but the only other places that have Electoral Colleges are India, Nepal, Pakistan, and Vatican City. In India the president doesn't count—it's a figurehead role; Pakistan is shady; Nepal is a country created for Instagram; and Vatican City, since its president is the pope, that turns the cardinals into the Senate, and, other than the College of Cardinals and the Swiss Guard, there are no citizens. Have you ever heard of a million-dollar listing in Vatican City? No. Because there's no real estate agent—you can't just live there.

The argument for an Electoral College is that if you got rid of it, the people would elect a populist WrestleMania-type personality but actually the opposite seems to have happened. The people didn't but the Electoral College did. So, I don't know what to tell you. Our system has a lot of dated ideas like . . .

THE SUPREME COURT

Nine old cranks who probably spend half their day showing each other pictures of their grandchildren. It was 9 people when we started this country and we only had 1 million people living here. Now we have 300 million people. So, we should have 270 Supreme Court justices. How about this? We treat the Supreme Court decisions with foul shots. Or we shoot the odd finger. Because their decisions affect 328 million people but are made by 9 people, appointed based on who dies when whichever party is in power. That doesn't sound very well thought out. We treat the Supreme Court justices with the idealistic innocence that only our country could have. They have to be fair and impartial. Nobody in history is impartial. Even on *Family Feud*, I bet Steve Harvey is always rooting for one family more.

TAXES

That's what made us blow up at England, and it's still the big issue. How much is the government (the taxpayer) obligated to help people? Everybody agrees the rich are out of control, but that's not really the conflict. The conflict is how socialist we are going to be. Everybody is a little bit socialist. And a little bit capitalist. But the degree is what we have been fighting over. And also, who is in charge of the system? States or the federal government? Even the state and federal governments aren't even really sure. Because the government is made up of people. And people are not that smart or that noble. You want the average government worker to spend their weekends thinking about how best they can serve the intentions of the founding fathers throughout their day at the Department of Commerce? I'm sure they start out that way. But then they find people to flirt with, or gossip with, or hate. And suddenly it's like every other job. How come he's got a window? How come they're allowed to get away with coming in late?

ELECTIONS

They're always held in an elementary school that brings back weird memories for everybody. Why not put them in bars? Why don't they make voting more like a Dave and Buster's? Instead of booths, a pop-a-shot basketball game where they have the two hoops and one is Democrat and one is Republican and you shoot for whoever you want and there's a chance you hit the wrong one. Keeps it exciting.

Instead of stupid "I Voted" buttons, they give you a drink ticket or rewards points at CVS.

THE DECLARATION OF INDEPENDENCE

Also, if we were gonna have slavery, the founders shouldn't have called it the Declaration of Independence—that led to a natural hypocrisy that didn't help us. Somebody, probably John Adams, questioned Jefferson:

JOHN ADAMS

Hey, man, do you wanna change this line about all men created equal?

JEFFERSON

Why?

ADAMS

Well, you have slaves.

JEFFERSON

So do you.

ADAMS

No, I don't. Nobody up here does.

JEFFERSON

You're kidding me.

Thomas Jefferson justified it probably by talking to the Southern contingent: "The British are up our ass. You want to talk about how I take care of my business or you want to be paying taxes to King George the Third! Love to see these Yankees come down and do what I do. In that heat. Walk a mile in my shoes. You goddamn right, Thomas. You know I'm right. You got George Washington up there, beloved, and acting like he ain't got slaves." The other Southern states were like, "You damn right." And that was that. The North made that deal with the devil, so to speak. They said, "We will give it time, and eventually they will stop the slavery."

They sacrificed slavery for the cause of survival against Britain. If they had said, "Screw it, we are breaking up," would the South have given in? Would the South have survived? We'll never know. The North gave in and the rest is a very racially charged history. And the history of mankind is saturated in slavery. The difference is they didn't promote their own Declaration of Independence at the same time. Our biggest problem is that there wasn't a line in the Declaration of Independence that said, "We hold these truths to be self-evident that all men are created equal"—and then maybe a parentheses, "(Yeah, we know what you are gonna say but just let us finish)"—"that they are endowed by their Creator . . . and I know it sounds like bullshit." I know it's a Band-Aid on cancer, but it couldn't have turned out worse. It's funny because the country really was—and is—great for a lot of people, but it's got that evil streak. It's Woody Allen. The guy's made some American masterpieces. So essentially, the Declaration of Independence was *Annie Hall*—it was brilliant but only enjoyed by white people.

The founding fathers were wedding planners. They made promises in the Constitution that no one can live up to. And our system wasn't completely set up to back up the founders' words. Because a representative democracy has a lot of flaws. Because there's the human factor to representation. They have to deal with hundreds of different needs and personalities in their districts. And a lot of unreasonable and mentally ill people and a lot of people with different degrees of power. It's like your wedding. You want everybody to have a good time. You plan the tables to make sure the people who hate each other don't sit too close to each other. You have to have vegan meals for Oregon and Vermont and bourbon for Tennessee and Kentucky, and you have to make sure Utah is not next to Florida. You have to be a good host and try to say hi to everybody, but ultimately you make sure that you spend time with the people with the biggest envelopes.

The other big flaw in the whole free speech thing was that it gave the human instinct to criticize an invitation to flourish. And now it's permeated the culture to the point where everybody that does anything is criticized: you mention any issue or situation, and the most common reaction is how it doesn't work. No one ever says, "It's complicated" or "We are doing pretty good considering the flaws that are inherent in any job." We made it our reflex to automatically blame the people who actually try to do something. Nobody criticizes people who sit home all day and work from their computer. No. It's only the people that have to go out and be seen. Ask anybody about any job and they will tell you what's wrong. Education? The teachers are not doing their job. Law enforcement? Cops are violent and racist. The unions? Greedy and corrupt. The government? A bloated, bureaucratic mess. Our foreign policy? Imperialism and exploitation. On trade? We're getting screwed by the rest of the world. The insurance companies? They're robbing us and leaving us to die. The entertainment industry? Opiate of the masses. The media? Propaganda and fake news. Sports? Toxic masculinity. Food industry? Poisoning us with genetic engineering. We hate everything. Except ourselves. That's the way the Bill of Rights is set up. You can insult anything that's part of the system. But you can't insult the people. Even during presidential debates, you will never hear one politician say, "I would like to make some systemic change, but look who I'm dealing with. You dumbasses. I don't trust you and I don't like you."

Philly always has been the East and Pittsburgh is the Midwest. Pittsburgh is where the fans are obsessed with the Steelers and Philly is where the fans are obsessed with themselves. Philly fans are famous for throwing snowballs at nuns and batteries at cancer survivors. They even had their own prison, originally called Veterans Stadium, which is an idea I wish would spread to comedy clubs. Philly and Pittsburgh are two cities that symbolize early American greatness. The foundation of our government started on the East Coast when all these brilliant guys threw out ideas for how the country should operate while dropping names like Cicero and John Locke and Demosthenes the way Philly people today drop DeSean Jackson and Carson Wentz. Then you've got Pittsburgh, which represents big business and blue-collar, hardworking Americans. They had the steel industry because Pittsburgh was where all the coal mines were. So, you had all these big Polish immigrants working the coal mines for the first big-billionaire tycoon, Andrew Carnegie. Andrew

Carnegie actually became a pretty good guy as bad guys go. He felt guilty after the Johnstown flood and the homestead strike, he only took $50,000 a year salary, and he spent most of the rest of his life as a philanthropist. He represented the dichotomy of the American invention that the robber barons gave us, the bipolar billionaire. But everybody thinks he was a psycho because it's a cooler story and the steel mills were rough, so you figure he had to be. Except he wasn't. But to this day you go to Pittsburgh and the surrounding areas and even Bethlehem, Allentown, etc. and there's a few guys that look like they drink at the Knights of Columbus and attended the wedding in *The Deer Hunter* and they look at you like, "You're not a man. You've never done a man's work unless you've shoveled coal into a blast furnace and then gone to a first communion in a Jack Lambert jersey."

Yeah, Pennsylvania is all the beauty and tragedy of the country. It's big, it's diverse, it's got people in research labs trying to cure diseases and people in meth labs trying to figure out where you can sell a garden hose that you stole from the feed store. Pennsylvania is every state. It's got economic disparity, racial tension, MAGA and progressives who hate each other, and a moderate majority made up of people just muddling along trying not to get killed, watching Netflix, and, once a month, taking out their frustration by ax throwing at the Fun Center while the kids are vaping in front of the rock climbing wall. Life is not all it's cracked up to be, but you gotta keep moving forward because you never know.

The Amish are also a big thing in Pennsylvania. I think about them a lot lately because of the internet. They still don't go for any of it. They still won't go online—no cell phones, no Instagram, no nothing. I used to think they were idiots, but the more we become a society that can't stop texting and tweeting and charging, the more the Amish seem like they are the smart ones and we are the idiots. They don't have feuds, people leaving six question marks when they don't answer a text, or the need to remember any passwords. They just happily churn butter and raise barns. I'm sure there's a couple of unhappy types there, though.

The kid who sucks at carpentry and the girl who doesn't look good in a bonnet. Every culture has those people. The people who just go a different way. The redneck who's a Bernie Bro. The black kid who likes Springsteen. The comedy fan who doesn't like Colin Quinn. Outliers. So, Pennsylvania gave us our system and we blew the world's mind. We were the Beatles. We changed the world and everybody was excited to see us, but we can break up with them too, and just like the Beatles we'll never be as good separately as we were together.

NEW JERSEY

NEW YORK'S STRAIGHT MAN

It's not easy to talk about New Jersey because everybody expects it to be insults all the time. New Jersey is actually a very culturally rich state. If you call tollbooths and traffic circles and exits on the wrong side culture. It's Italians that moved from the Bronx and spend most of their time at Formica tables at diners. It has the most diners of any state and it's referred to as the diner capital of the world. Why? Is it because people from New Jersey like to stare out windows? Or because they miss the stoops of the Bronx, where you could sit and talk with other people? Also, when you spend that much time in the car you get lonely, but that could apply to a lot of states. I mean demographically it's 45 percent Italian and 45 percent Indian and 10 percent everyone else. I don't know what attracted Italians and Indians to New Jersey. Maybe it's the spicy food. Maybe it's the software and technology. Is that racist? To say that Indians are into technology? When you call tech support, do they pick up in a German accent? My point is that people are drawn to certain things. Thomas Edison was a world-class nerd and the main street in Edison, New Jersey, is called Little India because India has a high nerd ratio.

People feel like they know New Jersey because of *The Sopranos* and *Jersey Shore*. Basically, the way we seem to know any place is by its portrayal. Then you go there and you go, "Hey, where's Snookie?" and the people there go, "There's no Snookie here; this is Princeton, for God's sake!" America's first seaside resort was Cape May. Before that, people only used the sea to fish or kill themselves. Then somebody went to Cape May to kill themselves and changed their minds and went home and said, "I actually enjoyed that time before and after. On the sand." And everybody said, "They really are crazy. Why would you lie on sand? You use the water and then get out." People didn't have time to lie on the sand. It seemed weird at first. Because it is kind of weird. It would be like if after you took a shower, you put on sunglasses and you laid on a towel on the bathroom floor and read a book for an hour.

The other resentment New Yorkers have against New Jersey is that we have to share so many things with them. The Statue of Liberty is New York land and Jersey water. The Holland Tunnel is half New York and half New Jersey. MetLife Stadium is the New York Jets and the New York Giants. We share a stadium! And the ironic thing is the Jets fans act more New Jersey than the Giants fans even though they're Jersey's team, even though they're called New York. It's hard to explain. New York is connected to New Jersey in this sick way. Only in the North. South Jersey is connected to Philadelphia. They even have that dumb accent and they like the Eagles and they just enjoy Philly. North Jersey has more of a New York accent, only they pronounce their *R*s more than they do in New York.

The United States is obviously all about real estate. And New Jersey was the first move west. That was the Wild West in 1650. The Lenape Tribe divided it first by turtle, wolf, and turkey. Clans. Today it would be divided by rest-stop areas. Peter Minuet called the state New Sweden and people would leave New Amsterdam (New York) and say, "I'm moving way out west to New Sweden." And people even then would ask, "What exit?" It's where Washington famously crossed the Delaware, which was considered a dangerous move because of the British and the ice and the Jersey drivers.

New Jersey always feels like it's lived in the shadow of New York (as it should). New Jersey's residents have always come to New York and we would make fun of their driving and their suburban way of looking at things. Every city has a suburb that it can do that to. A scapegoat. The place where the people come in on the weekends and you can feel superior. Everybody has people they want to feel superior to. That's how you bond. By having a common enemy. But for some reason one day in the early 1980s everybody started to attack New Jersey. Even people that never went near it started to make New Jersey jokes. I don't know why. Maybe they heard about the chemical-plant smell or whatever it was. New Jersey has the most toxic waste dumps in America. I don't know why. Maybe for getting rid of New York's waste. They are the garbage man for New York. But they also had the first baseball and basketball games. They had the first light bulb. They had the first phonograph, so they could listen to whoever was their version of Bruce back in 1880. And I have to say Bruce Springsteen really saved that state. Because he gave Jersey an identity. They were the state that was always in a muscle car on a drive to oblivion. And he gave them self-esteem. And they should have self-esteem. They were one of the original colonies! New Jersey was one of the original thirteen colonies, but people don't see it that way. There's nothing historical or colonial about it. The state just doesn't feel like part of that time period. For better or for worse. They seem like they just appeared fully formed around 1978. They've never had courtly manners. They are not refined. Having refineries does not count as being refined. They never had a landed gentry. Their philosophy has always been they've got to hold on to what they've got. It doesn't make a difference if they make it or not, they've got each other and that's a lot for love. They'll give it a shot.

MARYLAND

THE COUPLES' THERAPY STATE

Maryland is one of those states that everybody has been to for no real reason. I like the fact that they have a football team named after a famous poem. That's pretty classy. Playing a game where you have to be ready to break bones and kill and they say, "What are you named after? Eagle, Lion, Bear?" And Maryland says, "It's a narrative poem written by Edgar Allan Poe." And then they get down into a three-point stance for sixty minutes of macho brutality.

I actually heard that the chant before the Ravens leave the locker room is "Once upon a midnight dreary! Okay, let's go out there and rap at their chamber door!!" They also have a British flag design, which is a little bit of a move. They are like the girl that still follows her ex on social media just to keep her options open.

Maryland's got the navy, which is good because even though there's army and air force, the navy is still the one you have to go through to land in the actual country. That's how it's always been and there's something about that. Going out on the high seas to intercept some people who think they are going to land in your country and start pushing their weight around. Annapolis used to be the capital of the country, by the way, and it was known as "the Athens of America" in the 1700s.

The Mason-Dixon Line is right between Maryland and Pennsylvania, so technically they're in the South. Their state song is a tirade against Abraham Lincoln and the "Northern Scum." Wow, a little dated, huh. So their state song is not exactly patriotic. Everybody's gotta be aware of the changing times. I mean, even Aerosmith doesn't perform "Dude (Looks Like a Lady)" anymore. It's not what you would call patriotic, yet conversely the "The Star-Spangled Banner" was written fighting off the British in Baltimore's harbor. They are very conflicted. They love baseball, yet jousting is the state sport. They are very proud to be the home of crab cakes. Yet the crab cakes are imported. Obviously, Maryland has dual personality disorder. They don't know if they wanna be North or South, America or England, Annapolis or Baltimore. John Wilkes Booth or Harriet Tubman. John Waters or Cal Ripken Jr. Ira Glass or Sugar Ray Leonard. Are they sailing in the Chesapeake Bay or season 4 of *The Wire*? They are the conflicted part of our country's psyche. The contradictory nature of us. The people who voted for Bernie in the primary and then Trump in the general.

Maryland is where we should hold a soul-searching national therapy session. Where everybody lets out all their real feelings and people scream in each other's faces across the inner harbor. We'll have Civil War–style reenactments, only based on today's conflicts. Instead of blue versus gray uniforms, it's Starbucks versus Dunkin' Donuts uniforms. Both sides already have Civil War beards, both sides wear trucker hats—some worn ironically, some worn literally. And then we get into couples' therapy. "When you say I can't get married because I'm gay that makes me feel unsafe." "When you call me 'redneck' you make me feel less than." "OK, compromise, once a week for date night we agree to watch NASCAR, and once a week we agree to watch Florence and the Machine's Tiny Desk Concert."

NEW YORK

THE QUIET STATE WITH THE CITY THAT NEVER SHUTS UP

Before corona, New York City was a madhouse. Citi Bikes and parking and street carts and food trucks and cars and tour buses. Drilling, scaffolding. Sledgehammers. Paving trucks on side streets.

This city is one of those real housewives who spends all her time at the cosmetic surgeon. But every time she gets one thing done something else bothers her. This city has crow's-feet and we just need to accept that we're getting old. They've dug up my street four times since I moved here six years ago. What did you miss the first three times? It's pipes and wires and rock. They said they were working on the pipe on the left side. Now the other one is rusted. It's like a pulmonary surgeon who says, "I didn't notice last time you have another lung."

The Dutch bought it for $24. Manhattan only. Unlike most houses, they took it when it was open concept and subdivided it into a multifamily with 2 million rooms. Then you had the Hudson and the East River double sinks. But the point is that when you say New York, nobody even realizes what's going on upstate. People ignore it. In New York, like most states, you have the main city and then the suburbs and then the country and then the "other cities." The hometown high school football heroes that peaked and now they have to sit quietly in the local bar and talk about the glory days. Because all of these cities were superstars back in the day. Buffalo? Rochester? They were right on the Great Lakes!! If you wanted to trade, you had to go through them. Before planes, before railroads, it was all about the lakes. If you were lucky enough to live near a lake, you were set for life. Some cities just can't get a break. Like Rochester. They had Bausch + Lomb, Xerox, Kodak. They screwed up famously when they refused to go to digital, even though their research department came up with an early version. SONY took advantage. This is what happens. It happened too on the other side of the Great Lakes in Detroit with the auto industry. I think the lesson is don't take on the Japanese. You will lose every time. If the Japanese say they are going to go into your business, leave. If Japan decides to go into standup comedy tomorrow, I'll march right down to Astor Place and join the Blue Man Group. But that's what happened to Rochester.

Then you have Buffalo. They don't even know what their industry is. Now they just wait for the snowplows to finish up so they can enjoy those two weeks of spring. Used to be steel and shipping. Then you have Albany, which is supposedly the capital of New York. Of the Empire State! You go there and it's deserted all the time. You think I'm exaggerating. I've been there twenty times and I've never seen a person. That's how most downtowns are in America and it used to make me depressed but now I realize they were just social distancing before it was cool. Except for Boston, San Francisco, and Chicago, people are not on the streets downtown. Atlanta, Houston—they all claim to work downtown, but they must drive straight into underground garages and then leave at 5 o'clock. It's annoying. That's the thing about New York City. Yes, we are cocky and think we are the greatest, but you know what? Even Europeans bought apartments here, and you know what snobs they are. Even rich South Americans and Asians want to have a place here. You would be conceited too if everybody kept throwing money at you.

New York is the country's real estate salesperson. Let's face it. What is real estate after you've seen a place? You've got to resell it to the next generation. Old-fashioned real estate was you named it after you and then you owned it. So everything from the Bronx to Jacksonville was named after you. You or a saint. Everybody moved into packed tenements on the Lower East Side and Brooklyn—six to a room, overcharged by exploitive landlords—then they made enough to move out to the sanitary suburbs, and then their grandkids hated the antiseptic suburbs and moved back to the Lower East Side and Brooklyn—six to an apartment, with a greedy landlord. And now all the office buildings in Manhattan have emptied out because nobody goes to the office anymore—they work off their phones. So now the offices are becoming apartments for young people that are excited to move to New York. Now that Bushwick and Crown Heights are overrun they are back in Lower Manhattan in old office buildings.

In the beginning, the churches were the real estate company. They would buy it up and let people live near the church. They owned the real estate. If you wanted to make a deal, you had to go to church. "Bless me, Father, for I have sinned. I didn't realize the cap rate would change because the current market value didn't take into consideration the net operating income of the tea tax."

Started in the twentieth century, real estate in New York was actually simple. Follow the gays. You could walk around the neighborhood and ask a resident, "What'd you think of the Tonys last night?" If they say that Judith Light got robbed, you should invest.

In the old days, because of the mafia, you had to deal with all the unions. If you wanted to put up a high-rise, for the building permits, you had to go to a luncheonette in Lower Manhattan and talk to a guy from the Genovese family; for the cement, you had to go to a car service in Staten Island and talk to a guy from the Gambinos; for the plumbers to show up, you had to go to a candy store in Brooklyn and see the Colombos; for the environmental certificates, you had to meet a lawyer who worked in a storefront owned by the Luccheses in the Bronx; and for the air rights, you had to go to the "zoning board" at a pizza parlor in Queens.

New York is different now because of corona but its essence will never change. It's still the place you have to have. It's the party house. The place where everybody knows there's always something going on. You stop in and they are in the middle of something and they barely acknowledge you but they make you feel welcome. They don't smile, but they say, "Hey, the beer's in the fridge. Get it yourself. I'm cleaning up vomit in the street." And meanwhile the rest of the state is shaking its head and going, "I love them, but I don't know how they do it. I think about leaving them every day. I'd be happier with Pennsylvania or Ohio."

STATES VS. FEDERAL

States are like the local stores. The Federal Government is like Walmart, Amazon, etc. States are charming, and they are individual.

They make things by hand and they use locally grown products.

You can establish a personal connection, and if you have a problem, you can identify whom you need to address the problem to. And that store might be more inclined to care about you since you both live in the same area and it doesn't want to lose your business to another store. But it might not care that you have a problem at the same time; the downside is that they can be a little crazy, and if they don't like the way you look or the way you dress, they won't serve you. If they don't carry what you need, you have to go to another state to find what you want. They have store-by-store rules, and if you disobey one store's rules, you have to find another store and hope that one doesn't have a beef with how you act.

The big federal government store is impersonal and has that bland look to it. But it's also got a lot of people that have to answer to somebody, so they are more inclined to help. It sounds bad to be impersonal, but the upside is that there's efficiency. In the smaller state store, you've only got relatives working and some of them might be less qualified. The big store is heartless, but that's better for efficiency in some ways. But the big store also has investors just like big government has influence, so the customer/citizen is not necessarily its number one priority. We need the tension between state and federal. We need to be able to think for ourselves sometimes, and we need to be part of the collective at the same time. It's a delicate and complicated relationship in our country. States versus federal is another way of saying Mason versus Dixon.

$\bigstar$ $\bigstar$ $\bigstar$

THE SOUTH

*If you don't like the way I'm living, you just leave this
long-haired country boy alone.*
—CHARLIE DANIELS

The South and the North have always had different personalities. Always
have, they were settled by different types of people, and the weather and
the economy are not the same. When the South and the North found a
common enemy, it was supposed to bind us. It's true that people bond
by resentment against a third party, but it never lasts and eventually
you turn on each other. And the Constitution was to blame because the
founders didn't resolve any of these conflicts and acted like they could
put it off and it would work itself out. And so the South and the North
have been in an ugly marriage for a couple of hundred years. Full of
fights and ridicule and magical thinking and nobody is happy, but we're
stuck together for financial reasons. And yet nobody has any ideas about
how to fix it. Because: Fix what? That statement assumes people need
to fix their opinions, and fixing an opinion means agreeing with you.
That's the opposite of this country's reason for being founded, which
is to let you have your own opinion. You could have a say. You could
have a personality. Nobody in the feudal system was allowed to show

a personality. They had to keep it hidden. In America your geography sets your personality.

If you don't know the personalities of your society it will crumble. You have to know who the troublemakers are, who the salespeople are, who the politicians are, who the job creators are. And you need all these different types of people to make a nation function. And most important, you need the masses, the people who, when it's time to farm, don't ask questions but pick up a rake. When we need coal or minerals, they put on a hard hat. When you open a factory, they put on safety goggles. When a war starts, they put on a helmet and pick up a gun and get on a boat. Every society needs them. But the only thing you can't do to them is insult them and ridicule them and then expect them to keep their side of the bargain.

★ ★ ★

GEORGIA

HOLLYWOOD'S BOOTY CALL

Georgia was founded as a jail. But that's not that bad. A lot of good places started as prisons. Look at Australia. They started as a prison, and today they are not just a continent but a country. Who knows where Georgia goes from where it is today? Georgia was named after the iconic Englishman King George, not to be mistaken for iconic Englishman Boy George.

The whole state is covered in pollen, which is kind of weird. Nobody talks about it, but apparently there's nothing you can do about it but sit there and sneeze. I'd be interested to see how much allergy medication and Kleenex they sell down there. The number one phrase in Georgia is probably "Gesundheit." Everybody's sleeve is probably covered in mucus too. It's the peach state, but also number one in peanuts and pecans and Vidalia onion producers who say that their onions are the sweetest in the world. Which is fine, but who eats onions to satisfy a sweet tooth? You ever see onions in an Easter basket? Exactly.

R.E.M. They are a big part of Georgia. That's the thing in the South. They always have that college town with the band that makes it big. Hootie and the Blowfish in South Carolina. It's for the other college kids. It's the section of the college where they don't talk about the "dawgs" except ironically. Not that the R.E.M. kids of the 80s wouldn't be horrified to be put in the same category as the frat boys of the 90s that liked Hootie. And even talking about college rock feels like a quaint walk through the past. There's just mainstream saturation of everything. So that anytime a band comes out with anything decent, twenty other bands steal it before it goes viral. That's why people laugh at hipsters saying, "I knew them before everybody else." That used to mean the general public. Now it means the other bands.

And now that I think about it, R.E.M. was the first hipster band. They were emo-ish but not depressed enough or self-destructive enough to be really emo. And they and their fans were kind of snobbish and at the same time compassionate. And a little nerdy. And they opened up the door for that whole nerd-rock movement with They Might Be Giants and Weezer, etc.

But back to Georgia, the number one producer of peanuts. Georgian Jimmy Carter was a peanut farmer and a president. I don't know a lot about farming, but I can't even picture peanuts being farmed. What, do you pick them? Do they grow in the ground? On trees? In some kind of leaf? I always think of peanuts as more of a nocturnal food. Picked at by divorced dads during happy hour at hotel bars. It seems like they are about as much a part of nature as maraschino cherries.

Then you have Atlanta. General Sherman burned it down during the Civil War. *After* he conquered it, which was a pretty messed-up move. You win and then you go, "Burn it." I mean, even in war there's got to be some class. It's like when somebody kicks your ass and then you're lying there and they kick you some more. Why???? You think you're cool showing everybody how coldhearted you are? Fine. If you're twelve. But General Sherman was a hallucinating, suicidal half-psychopath. He fought in every big battle in the war, and he was the hero in half and the goat in the other half. "Goat" in the old sense, not "greatest of all time." Goat used to be the opposite of greatest of all time. I don't know who changed it.

Goats are probably pleased to know they've been rebranded. But Sherman had PTSD and he was wounded twice and had three horses shot out from underneath him. By the time he reached Atlanta, you weren't getting Marianne Williamson.

Georgia also invented Coca-Cola. Which is the iconic American product. Anywhere you go, people have Coca-Cola. When I see the sign, I get happy. It's one of the greatest signs of all times. It's like driving down a highway and suddenly there's a big billboard with a picture of your grandma on it. I love Coca-Cola. Everybody loves Coca-Cola. Even in countries where they riot against American imperialism and Western influence and attack embassies and anything American, they never touch McDonald's or Coca-Cola signs.

Georgia's another one of those states where there's a lot of drama every election. Because it's liberal and it's conservative. And after Bill 481 on abortion got signed, Hollywood tried to boycott filming in the state. But to make the people of the state pay for the political act of the people in charge is a little strange. It's supposed to make the people rise up, I guess? Like sanctions in Iran or something. Only nobody else really ever does what you want them to. Unless you are giving them a job directly, people aren't going to back you—why would they? Show business people that are always out proselytizing are like the Christian missionaries that get beheaded in South Sea Islands. They don't understand that nobody wants them to decide what's the right thing for them. They don't actually get beheaded, but people just spend less time watching them. Most people in the "red state" frame of mind don't even watch Hollywood entertainment anymore. And at a time when entertainment is saturated with millions of streaming services. It's a weird time in this country.

Georgia tries to attract Hollywood because they want work and money even though they hate Hollywood, and then Hollywood comes in because they want tax breaks even though they hate Georgia. But maybe that's part of what Georgia represents. The complicated contradictory relationship America has with art vs. commerce vs. ideology vs. culture.

★★★ VIRGINIA

VIRGINIA IS FOR SMOKERS

Named after the Virgin Queen. Elizabeth the First. I'm sure she really appreciated that. Having her business put out in the street like that. Being nicknamed a virgin queen. It's humiliating. If you can't get laid as the queen, that's pretty low. You're telling me there wasn't one nobleman who was willing to get in there and do it and become the king? That's bad. That's an insult. That's the difference between men and women. Because I'm sure there were kings just as ugly as Elizabeth, but there was some female member of the royal court who was like, "Hey, I'll close my eyes and wake up as the queen." Look at Hugh Hefner. He was a bag of skin the last twenty years of his life, but a couple of Playmates would draw straws every night to see who was going to hold their breath and take one for the team. I bet every one of the Playmates in the last fifteen years of Hugh Hefner's life cursed the invention of erectile-dysfunction pharmaceuticals.

The first place people landed in America was Jamestown, in what became Virginia. Jamestown was established as a silk-trading center. But a fungus destroyed the mulberry bushes, so they planted tobacco. They should've called their state Smoke and Silk, am I right? Pretty cool for an album from the early 60s—maybe a duet album with Mel Tormé and Dinah Washington. But instead the settlers chose to name it after a virgin—I guess since it was the first settlement, they figured it was virgin territory. But obviously it wasn't the first settlement and they weren't the first settlers. There were native people living there. And when the Jamestown people first arrived, the native settlers said, "Who are you?" and the Jamestown people said, "We're the first settlers." And the native people said, "But if we're here, how can you be the first settlers?" And the Jamestown people said, "But what if you weren't here?"

The big American sins to answer for started in Virginia, sure, but this book is not the Hague. It's supposed to be funny, but it's not gonna bring closure to people. But slavery started in Virginia. The first English colony was Virginia, and Virginians had slaves. But slavery spread all over immediately, even to New York City and New England. Virginia was the original sin on that one, and it spread down south a lot easier than up north. Everyone says this was because the South was agricultural and the North was industrial, but there were a lot of factories down south and a lot of farms up north. Some say it's because the Puritans were more into the morality of Christianity and considered slavery wrong because of it, but the South was pretty Christian too. Still is. So maybe it was the weather. Or maybe it was the people. For whatever reasons, that's how it ended up and how the South became known for slavery.

The South was about farming and honor killing. They were from that British tradition of duels, and most duels were Southern. They were easily insulted. They spoke the most flowery language, and they probably felt the most embarrassed about being a slave economy. You know how when you are doing something wrong, you start to see how everybody else is wronger than you? That might have been why there was so much gunplay down there. Also, the slaves were doing all the work, so you'd have time on your hands. Which can also lead to too much time thinking about those microaggressions. You're sitting there with a bourbon and lemonade and you start to say, "I didn't appreciate Elbridge making that little crack about our dogwood trees. My wife is proud of them and it's disrespectful to try to be funny about my backyard." Next thing you know, it's 5:30 A.M. and you've got a loaded gun in your hand.

Eight presidents were born in Virginia. It's one of those things. People tell their kids, "You could grow up and become president one day," and in Virginia it's the truth. Virginia's got quite the history. All thirteen colonies do, but Virginia and Massachusetts really run it into the ground. Virginia acts like they invented the government all on their own, and Massachusetts acts like they fought the Revolutionary War by themselves. Half the battles were fought in Virginia. Probably because it's convenient. Even in wartime, it's location, location, location.

The American Revolution ended with the surrender of General Charles Cornwallis in Yorktown. Then Robert E. Lee surrendered at Richmond in the Civil War. Virginia's a good place to surrender, I guess. It's also a pretty place. I always think of Virginia as being a bunch of beautiful lawns and a bunch of colleges where they all know the government inside and out. You know the professors have bow ties and every student looks like they just ironed their khaki shorts. It's one of those polite states. Nobody curses in Virginia. If you want to curse, you go over the border to West Virginia and you can curse up a storm. They have cursing blue laws. Virginia doesn't curse. It's refined. It's stately. It's delicate.

Then you have Northern Virginia, which is just the backyard of Washington, D.C.: CIA and NSA and FBI. Acronym country. It's the kind of area where all the guys part their hair to the side and their wives all secretly smoke. There are a lot of secrets hidden in those split-level broken homes. I always feel bad for the CIA, because the FBI are always the good guys in the movie and the CIA are the bad guys. In any movie where the local rogue cop has to battle the FBI and the CIA, by the end the FBI guy is pretty cool but the CIA guy is literally the head of whatever crime group they are up against. It's always that same kind of bland white guy that represents evil in Hollywood. He's calm and quiet and in the last scene he kills twelve people—because it's not enough that he poisoned the rain forest and destroyed an entire village. They want to make sure people realize he's the bad guy by having him mow down the hero cop's neighbors and six detectives so that there's no doubt who he is. And in all the Jason Bourne and Jack Reacher movies. The CIA is evil except for the one rogue agent and the one tech nerd who helps him. They built entire movie franchises against them. I would like to see *one* movie where the CIA is the hero. They go up against the evil forces of a local cop and the FBI and the indigenous people of some third world country, and the CIA kills them all but they turn out to be right for some reason. Yes, I'm the only person that feels bad for CIA agents.

But, of course, it all comes back to 1619 and the beginning of the slave trade in the United States. We got off on the wrong foot. And everybody knows it. But where do we go from here? That's the part nobody wants to talk about. Reparations aren't going to happen. How do you deal with legacy, history? We should've had a full-out race war in the 60s. Everybody could've gotten it out of their systems. We were on our way to having one, but we got sidetracked by Vietnam. In fact, maybe subconsciously that's why we went into Vietnam. We should've had a quick race war. And it's too late now. Because there's so many other ethnic groups and many more people are multiracial. You would have to do 23 and Me before shooting someone. You'd have to say, "I'm going to shoot you, but first spit in this cup." Then wait a few weeks. Thank God. I almost killed my second cousin on my mother's side. So instead we have white guilt and black resentment. And we go on and on.

We should have a racial conversation once a month, like a constitutional convention. In Virginia, in the spot where the first slave ship landed. Go back to where the problem first started. And that spot would be considered territory where you are allowed to speak freely with no repercussions. Like the ships where you can gamble at the three-mile limit.

★ ★ ★
SOUTH CAROLINA

TOUCHY LITTLE BUGGER

South Carolina is one of those states that has always been causing drama. It was where the first shots were fired in the Civil War. It was the first state to secede during the Civil War. Then it was three weeks before the next state seceded. That was probably a nervous three weeks for South Carolina. They thought, "Oh shit, did we not read the room?"

It could've been South Carolina against the whole country. The rest of the South made them sweat. Not that they weren't already sweating since it was the South. The other Southern states probably didn't like them because they are snobs or at least they have that snobbish element. Like sitting on the big porches with a cup of tea, while one of the daughters is playing a cello. That's what South Carolina is. What they call the "genteel South," a little more aristocratic than the rest of the South. They would like to enjoy an art exhibit or something along those lines. Rudeness was a major crime. If someone took offense, everybody in the county would hear about it. It was similar to today's politically correct society in terms of sensitivity, only it was anything but politically correct, obviously. Instead of people taking offense at someone saying something racist, people would be offended if you said something that wasn't racist. But it was the same basic idea. Which is pearl clutching (in South Carolina's case, literally) and gasps of shock over someone saying something off message.

Yes, South Carolina was a state of sharecroppers, rednecks, and Scarlett O'Hara types who spent their time going to garden parties, and cotillions, meetings and having affairs with authors and not noticing the authors were gay and then having tea and biscuits and fainting. Smelling salts were probably big in South Carolina until about six years ago. The point is that South Carolina harbors true believers when it comes to the Confederacy. Eight counties still celebrate Confederate Memorial Day. I didn't even know there *was* a Confederate Memorial Day.

Also, you had Charleston, which is part of the liberal South, along with Austin, Texas, and Athens, Georgia. These are places where people vote for Democrats and where the kid in the family that hates tailgate parties moves after high school. They have a lot of art schools and coffee shops, and there are no theme bars or sports paraphernalia stores. If you want an artisanal beer in South Carolina, you have to go to Charleston.

Myrtle Beach is known as the Redneck Riviera, and it's got the souvenir stores with the "funny" T-shirts like FUNCLE ("fun uncle") and SOS ("seniors on spring break"); the Putt-Putt; the tattoo parlors; the outlaw bikers; the odd serial killer before he gets famous. Then they have those islands off the coast that were isolated from the mainland for hundreds of years with the Gullah Geechee people. Everybody in South Carolina is a little bit exotic. Even the Marshall Tucker Band was a little different because most southern rock bands wouldn't open their set with a five-minute flute solo.

Like Virginia, South Carolina is a little bit of an anglophile. They still like bow ties and debutante balls and polo matches. They drink tea in the gazebo. They are all about the lawn. It's all about the landscaping. Everybody's got beekeepers' masks and gardening gloves. It's all about showing off your prize petunias and not getting sunstroke. When you're in South Carolina, you feel like you need to brush up on your manners. You don't know which fork to use or how big of a sip to take of your iced tea. You don't want to visit them often because it's uncomfortable, but they do set the table pretty nicely. It's like dinner at Martha Stewart's house.

NORTH CAROLINA

AMERICA'S ASHTRAY

They are southern, but they love basketball more than football. Every school—Duke, NC State, UNC—okay, Wake Forest likes football, but nobody asked them. They go along to get along. North Carolina is the South but it's also the tech South. It's been said that Raleigh-Durham has the highest concentration of nerds outside of Comic Con. Or at least I'm saying it right now. North Carolina nerds. Math labs and meth labs. They've also got the hippie South. Like Asheville. You go to Asheville and they eat organic roadkill. It's the only place they roast hogs in patchouli oil. Nobody shaves and everybody's barefoot. Kind of like West Virginia, only nobody in West Virginia can pronounce Ray LaMontagne.

But the main thing about North Carolina is smoking. If you look at the entire United States, it's all about real estate. So when North Carolina had tobacco, back when everyone smoked, they were prime commercial real estate. Virginia too, but they had other things going on and the mighty leaf was all North Carolina had to boast about. Kids smoked in playgrounds; the whole state was encouraged to smoke. If you didn't, it was like ordering rice in Idaho. Have a goddamn potato, keep us going. They probably hate rice in Idaho. Just like they hate the antismoking laws in North Carolina.

They are the weirdest bastards you'd ever want to meet. They named Raleigh after Sir Walter Raleigh, who was known mainly for smoking. He was the world's first smoker. In fact, that's how tobacco ended up in America. He took cigarettes back to England, lit one up, and they said, "I'm sorry, you can't stay in here with that. You have to go outside." And by "here" they meant all of Europe, and by outside they meant across the Atlantic. But then they started thinking about it and remembered Sir Walter looked pretty cool doing it. So they invited him back but told him to bring a few cartons. He did, but that started the Great Fire of London because they hadn't invented ashtrays yet. Sir Walter Raleigh must've had a lot of juice in England, though. Because he actually lost a colony full of English people and didn't get punished for it. He left them on Roanoke to go home, and when he came back there was no trace of them. Then he went to the local Native Americans and asked the chief, and he spoke to his warriors, and they probably gave him the old Ray Liotta when Paul Sorvino asks him about Billy Batts: "Nobody knows what happened. He came in the joint that night and then just disappeared." How do you lose a colony? And then they still let you be in charge. That's how it was in those days. If you were big in the colonies and the money was coming in, they didn't question it too closely.

North Carolina is also known as the state that knows how to talk to South Carolina. Whenever South Carolina gets heated about something, good old NC steps in.

NC
Hey, look at me. It's gonna be all right.

SC
Oh bullshit!! I'm fixing to ex-plode!!

NC

Trust me, it'll blow over.

SC

Washington's trying to mess me over again!

NC

Hey, they can't mess you over without messing me over, right?
And we stick together, okay?

SC

Umm . . . okay. Thanks for talking me down. I almost did
something crazy. Thanks, brother. Brothers for life?

NC

Brothers for life! Same last name, right?

The NASCAR Hall of Fame is in North Carolina. Probably because Dale Earnhardt is from there. The Intimidator!! He died on the track at the Daytona 500 like a man. Like I would like to die onstage at the Comedy Cellar and then have Jim Norton have to follow me. And I'll be on a cloud watching him bomb as he tries to make some "edgy" joke about my death and the crowd just stares at him.

The Wright brothers also started flight in North Carolina. That's pretty amazing. They really changed the game with that one. Probably at the first flight all the birds were like, "This is not good. We need to put a stop to this." But they just kept on keeping on. The birds probably had to reroute a lot of their flights just to deal with the "new kid in town." The swallows made an announcement: "All flights to Capistrano are now being delayed. We are sorry for the inconvenience." It's funny when we disrupt nature. They certainly have no trouble disrupting us. Pigeons have ruined more statues in New York than Antifa. And the

Wright brothers didn't even get that rich, when you think about it. But they probably didn't care; they were nuts anyway. Everybody got married in those days, but not these two "confirmed bachelors." Not that there's anything wrong with that. Wilbur died in 1912 of typhoid from bad shellfish, which I don't quite get—in those days people were supposed to be so tough; meanwhile, I would never get taken down by a shrimp scampi. And then Orville stopped talking to their sister because she got married, so obviously the Wright brothers had some freaky family things going on. Not to disparage their legacy, but he had a little bit of the old Cersei–Jaime Lannister thing happening.

So, North Carolina is beautiful but every time anyone in the world has to get a chest X-ray, they can thank North Carolina.

★ ★ ★

KENTUCKY

CARBON FACE PRINT

Kentucky is one of those states that you feel like it's a bunch of hollers and back roads and chimneys on those little houses. When I was a kid, we had all these cartoons like Snuffy Smith and Li'l Abner that basically made light of the brutal poverty of Appalachia. But people would laugh, because in those days you would punch down and up and body punch and kidney punch and rabbit punch. It didn't matter as long as you were punching. And comedy is not really punching anyway, and I can't emphasize that enough. In any case, Kentucky is one of those places that seems like you can't really hurt with punches because they don't feel them. They all have leather skin after the age of fourteen and they all still smoke because what's-the-difference-the-coal-mine's-going-to-get-you-anyways and they all have those long fingers and protruding Adam's apples. And the women all have those long dresses with the aprons on and they know how to skin a squirrel and they all have their hair pulled back in a bun. Even Neil Diamond's song "Kentucky Woman" goes "Well, she ain't the kind / Makes heads turn at the drop of her name / But something inside / That she's got turns you on just the same" . . . wow. It's a song. So, we don't see her. We only have Neil's description of this theoretical Kentucky woman. And you have to get all by the book and say, "Well, she's not that hot, but there's something about her." She's an imaginary woman, Neil, you hairy-chested buffoon. Just let her be beautiful for the sake of the state! Nobody needs the honest-to-a-fault Neil Diamond song. Hey, for that matter, why don't you change "Sweet Caroline" to "Fake-Nice Caroline" because—guess what, Neil—we cut you a lot of slack because the Band signed off on you by having you in *The Last Waltz* and everybody was afraid to say, "Neil Diamond? Isn't he kind of a cheeseball?" But now you are pushing it with this "Kentucky Woman" song, so try and keep below the radar and me and you can live and let the other live.

If there's one state that everybody thinks they know, it's Kentucky. The people there just seem very specific. They are what Hunter Thompson and Nelson Algren called "link-horns." Kentucky was settled by the offspring of indentured servants who came out of the British Isles and worked for a few years as bonded laborers. They were freed when their contract was finished and are what are called hillbillies today. Everybody makes jokes about hillbillies, but I've spent time in Kentucky and I have to say that I didn't see that many hillbillies.

I was at a comedy club in Lexington and saw a University of Kentucky basketball game. Ashley Judd was at the game and she looked up in the stands and saw me and she had that look on her face like, "What's this guy doing way up there? He's kinda famous, too." I didn't want to tell her how it is to be a comedian—it's a different kind of famous, where you don't get to sit on the floor; the owner of the comedy club has to get you in to the game and you sit in the blue seats and are lucky to be there. But it was a blast. Basketball is big in Kentucky. They love B-ball. Maybe because all those Appalachians are too skinny for football. It's basketball, then horses, then bluegrass music. Bluegrass is another one of those music forms you're not allowed to not like. Pretty annoying, but I don't make the rules of society; I just follow them. So when people mention Bill Monroe or Ricky Skaggs, I don't argue; I just nod my head like "great." Because, really, what do I know? I'm not a music expert. I know a lot about comedy, but that's about it. You have to go along to get along.

They've got a pretty good celebrity roster in Kentucky. George Clooney—although it bugs me, because I can just hear him saying, "Well, back in Kentucky we say that horse don't run on a muddy track" while he's sitting on his yacht in Lake Como. Then Muhammad Ali and Loretta Lynn—I'm sure *their* families would've gotten along way back when. Then you have Ned Beatty, who probably got flashbacks when they were shooting that scene in *Deliverance*. That's one of those scenes that I bet to this day he was hoping ended up on the cutting room floor. Because, let's face it, I don't care what kind of an artist you are, you don't want to see yourself being sodomized by a couple of toothless maniacs (or by anybody, really) on a thirty-foot screen.

But Kentucky's biggest star of all time is . . . Abraham Lincoln. Arguably the greatest president ever. Ended slavery and won the Civil War. Everybody loved him. Almost everybody. Then he goes to see a play and gets killed by John Wilkes Booth. Who shot Lincoln in the back of the head like Joe Pesci in *Goodfellas* and yelled, *"Sic semper tyrannis,"* which was what Brutus said at Caesar's assassination and which is also the Virginia state motto. It's better than if he yelled, "Virginia is for lovers!" I guess. *Sic semper tyrannis* is still the motto of Virginia, which is pretty disrespectful, but I guess they just didn't want to have all the plaques reset. I feel like when you think about democracy that's one of the problems. You get a guy like John Wilkes Booth and he feels he has the right to kill the president of the United States because in his "opinion" the president is wrong. At least in the old days if the king got assassinated it was by somebody on the inside who was trying to take his place. In democracy you can get killed and it has nothing to do with a power move. It's just a thing where they are saying, "We are equal, so my opinion must be heard." And I mean I know that's the point of this country, but is it really what we wanted? So that the second-best actor in the Booth family feels as if he can act out that he's equal to Abraham Lincoln? Maybe the greatest president of all time? But that's democracy in its purest form.

I saw a news story about how they are banning prayer lockers in Kentucky because of church/state separation. Just the fact that they have prayer lockers should tell you how we are never going to get together as a country. Kentucky has lockers where high school kids go to pray and California has safe-space lockers and Chicago has gang lockers. America's just a high school of wildly differing lockers and cultures. The answer is Catholic school. Everybody dresses the same, has the same classes, and behaves the same. Then when they get out, they have something to rebel against. A common enemy. You have to unite with division. People who have freedom growing up have nowhere to go as adults. You can only bond with others by common experiences from the past. And people in our country don't have a common past. Either it was brutal exploitation and oppression or a beacon of light and civilization in a primitive world. Why can't it be both? It *was* both! Like Catholic school itself!

Because Kentucky's not going to change and neither are you.

★ ★ ★

TENNESSEE

YOU'RE SO PRETTY, WHY DO YOU WEAR SO MUCH MAKEUP?

The original settlers broke the law by going to Tennessee. It was supposed to be only for the Cherokees. The English proclamation said that settlers were forbidden to move west of the Appalachians. So early Tennesseans were either really desperate or had a shit attitude. Or half of them were desperate and half of them had a shit attitude. But they wanted to become a state so that the feds would help them fight the Cherokees, and that's what happened. Becoming a state was the only way to get a fort and some troops. And it was one of those unwritten rules that people started to understand by looking at Tennessee. You wanted statehood, you had to shed a little blood, get a natural resource that could generate income—and in a couple of decades, we bring you in. We flag you. Get you a star. And once a state had that star, nobody could mess with it. No tribe, no other country, even the animals noticed you walked a little different. So Tennessee came into being and then Martin Van Buren (who in my opinion doesn't get enough credit for being kind of a prick) forced all the Cherokees out of their homes and onto the Trail of Tears to Oklahoma.

Nashville is an important part of the South because they're the Red State Network. They are the HBO, Netflix, Amazon, Hulu, Spotify, Apple Music for the entire South. I don't know if it's Tennessee's attitude that lets it be the home of country music. Country music is the South's only show business communication. There aren't really Southern TV shows—maybe a few, but they're written by northerners. They don't really have what you call representation in the movie and TV world. There are occasional examples like *Friday Night Lights* or some reality show with duck hunters, but for the most part the sections of our country are on different pages. Which is strange. We pretend to be unified, but we're actually not on the same page. And show business is the greatest reflection of that. It's always been like that a little bit, I guess, but now it's much more pronounced. Because movies and TV are an LA and New York thing, and so most of the people in charge are from the coasts. Or they have left the heartland to get away from it because they didn't like it. So now when people are all trying to tell their own stories, you have a whole bunch of places that have just completely dissociated from the television and movie industry. They will watch news or go to websites, and once in a while they'll watch some show through word of mouth, but in general, they know that they'll be the punch line in most of the comedy shows and they'll be the villain in most of the dramas. So, the only area where red states and blue states still pretend to get along is music. Whenever it's the Grammys or the American Music Awards—in all those music shows there's always a country music artist who does a song and the crowd is respectful, but you never see them at the after party. It's all fake. I think it's natural to have a cultural divide, but we still live with that pride that we are all Americans and we have to find places to meet. And we're not doing a very good job of it. We can't give up the idea of being the United States, but it's like one of those marriages where you wake up one day and you are lying in bed with a stranger. And you think, "Did I ever really even know this person? Or was I just projecting what I wanted them to be?"

★ ★ ★

LOUISIANA

THE BRAZIL OF AMERICA

We are a nation of laws. Common civil law. State law. Federal law. Constitutional law. Louisiana has Napoleonic code. Napoleonic code started with Napoleon, obviously. Because Louisiana makes up their own laws, they make up their own languages. They don't speak English, they speak French with a Brooklyn accent. Napoleonic law said, "You must be this tall to be emperor." There's no precedent allowed. If you bring up a case that's similar, they tell you, "That's not how we do it." "We don't want to hear somebody's opinion. We want to hear the law's opinion." "Hell, I don't know that judge! He might be a drunk fool best as I know." It's a state that you can't figure out because everybody's up to something. Louisianans wear masks literally and figuratively. They give you a drink when you cross the border and they keep you drunk the whole time. And they put mild hallucinogens in the food. Everybody is crazy everywhere, but in Louisiana they *know* they are crazy, and I guess that's a good thing. Everybody's playing zydeco Cajun swamp pop. Louisiana has always been an exotic place. It's like, what Vegas tries to be, Louisiana is naturally. Houseboats and gold teeth and fat guys with fishing hats. "What happens in Louisiana, stays in Louisiana" is not their motto. Their motto is, "Three can keep a secret if two are dead."

Louisiana is known for its partying, of course. The drinking age is 12 and one of the great hobbies is watching young children stumble into school on Monday morning after a weekend of heavy drinking. It's the only state where you are required by law to walk the street with an open container under the "Don't Kill the Buzz" statute. If you order a club soda, they ask you to leave the state. It's the only state where even the church services are held at night outdoors. It's not a state. It's a moveable feast.

One time I landed at the airport and the cabdriver, who was at least 400 pounds, stopped halfway through the trip and made me get out and pump gas while he went into the store to pay and pick up some goodies! And came out with a six-pack of beer. And opened one while he was driving me. And offered me one. And it was 10:30 A.M. That's New Orleans.

Sex, decadence, magic potions, corruption. Everybody is sweating and wearing Ray-Bans and plotting against each other. Bribery is still the system there. If you walk into a restaurant, there's a cash register and then there's the other cash register. And then there's envelopes for the police, the health inspector, the city planners. Every house has a list of names in their safe so nothing happens to them. You go to the bank, they bury the money in the backyard. How much you need? They have to go in the back and dig it up. Every parish has their own bank. They love gumbo and bouillabaisse because everybody's pansexual, multilingual, French, Spanish Black, and Indian. It's got that typical Huey-Long-and-back-alley-French-transsexuals-in-masks-with-little-cakes-typical-in-swamps-with-alligators-and-Cajuns-with-Brooklyn-accents vibe.

★ ★ ★

MISSISSIPPI

THE REDNECK'S REDNECK

Okay, you want the truth? Everybody's scared of you. Even the rest of the South is kind of freaked out by you. Your reputation is "the crazy redneck." The only ones that kind of don't worry about you are Alabama and parts of Tennessee. Mississippi became famous during the civil rights era, of course. Most of the shootings and bombings were in Mississippi and Alabama. Georgia probably loved it. They were like, "Sure, we can be a little bit racist, but these guys . . ." People like to put Mississippi out there as the scapegoat for all the racial drama in the country. Meanwhile every state has had racial tension in different ways since the beginning. Mississippi is just more upfront about it. So it's kind of what they're known for now. Like Idaho potatoes or Hawaiian pineapples. It's part of their identity. Once that's how people know you, then that's it. You have only one chance to make a first impression.

Elvis was from Mississippi. And he's famous for being from Mississippi. But he moved to Memphis when he was 12. I think we have to make new rules: If you moved before middle school, you are not from there. I'm sorry, Mississippi. But you have a lot of other famous people. Tennessee has nobody. So, how about a little charity? I know you've had a hard go of it. And the last thing you need is to lose Elvis. But I'm trying to set some rules about people saying where they are from. You know how many people I've met that say they're from Brooklyn and they moved when they were a year old? It's annoying. But I get it—Elvis is a big deal. How about this: Wherever you hit puberty is where you are from.

Mississippi is also home to those Gulf Coast casinos. That's where the real old-school gambling began. On those Mississippi riverboats. You had these guys playing with giant stickpins and pocket watches attached on a chain and they had giant mustaches. They would try to get all the rubes that were just traveling to buy dry goods or whatever. And they would strike up a conversation with you and then say, "You want to play a friendly game?" And if you said, "Yes," you ended up having to swim back home with empty pockets. They were hustlers. Some of them were cheaters, but if the riverboat caught you cheating, they'd chop off your fingers and feed them to the catfish in the mighty Mississippi.

Mississippi is also the home of Jimmy Buffet. Jimmy Buffet is the most American success story ever. He was a one-hit wonder who built an entire following around the idea of retirement and drinking margaritas. And these people follow him forever. He looked around and said, "What if there was a Phish for guys with gray goatees and fun cat ladies?" All the legendary American musicians that inspired the Beatles and the Stones and Dylan are from Mississippi. Muddy Waters and Howlin' Wolf and B. B. King and all these other blues musicians that you have to say you like or everybody considers you a musical idiot. I remember I bought this whole CD box set of Robert Johnson, another Mississippi blues legend, and one of my old friends Lou came over and saw it. He then proceeded to destroy my purchase, pointing out that I never liked that kind of music and I was a posturing phony for buying it and I probably didn't even listen to it. I wish I could say that I defended myself against Lou's slanderous and unwarranted attack. Unfortunately, Lou was accurate. I had done all those things in a midtwenties attempt to improve myself musically, and I had listened to two songs and then I felt tired. Blues songs make me feel like taking a nap. And when someone is riffing on the guitar in the middle of what should be a three-minute song for an extended period of time, I'm not screaming in ecstasy or waving my drink around or high-fiving other embarrassing people. I am just sitting there looking at my phone and hoping for a sweet release in the form of a building collapse.

Mississippi is also where Oprah is from. And William Faulkner. Although I can't imagine William Faulkner getting an Oprah book club selection and then signing for the soccer moms and they ask him how he stays so thin. And he says, "Emphysemalcholistictuberculosis."

So if the country is a street, then Mississippi is the house where the front porch is a little paint-chipped and one of the cushions is missing from the porch swing and the screen is patched up and the light is out and there's just four generations of eyes staring at a bug zapper.

$$\star \; \bigstar \; \star$$

ALABAMA

THREE YARDS AND A CLOUD OF DUST

Alabama is football. Everybody down south and in the Midwest loves football, but Alabama is the only state where the kids are bred to play. In other states, moms don't set up playdates with strength-and-conditioning coaches when the kid is seven. It's got a cool name as states go. Alabama. Then the people from there say, "Bama." Which ruins it for me. But they are very polite in the way they speak. They say hello by saying, "Hey," but they drag it out. "Haiy!" And they talk to you like you are a little kid. "Can I help you?" And they always say common things like you never heard of them. Why did they close the place. "They had a fire?" Yes, I'm familiar with fire. "So, it burned down?" Yeah, I know that's usually the end result of a fire. Stop talking down to me. When I was in Iraq, I was hanging out with a kid from Alabama who had the thickest accent and used all those expressions, like, "You can't pluck a chicken in a hen house." There's always an analogy which basically means people are gonna do what they're gonna do, like, "Kick a frog in the ass, he ain't gonna jump higher." It's always a physical interaction with a strange creature, like cursing at muskrats, kicking june bugs, or punching turtles. And it's all about Alabama and Auburn. You may think it's a friendly rivalry. It's not. One guy poisoned a tree that had been in Auburn for 150 years. He said he did it as a joke, "Hey, I heard about your great comedy act where you killed a hundred-year-old weeping willow." "Well, wait till you hear my closer where I poison the town's drinking supply."

The civil rights movement jumped off in Alabama, of course. The sanitation workers went on strike and then Rosa Parks. She wouldn't give up her seat on the bus. She was the second woman to do that. The first was named Claudette Colvin. She was a fifteen-year-old girl who got arrested for the same thing Rosa Parks did, only nine months earlier! But they didn't go with her because she was pregnant and they thought it was bad optics—as we say these days—to have an unwed mother be the symbol. Even though being pregnant would've offset that, because who needs to sit down more than a pregnant woman? (You wouldn't know that from the chivalrous New York City subway passengers, but still. . . .) Anyway, I was not a deciding vote of the Student Non-violent Coordinating Committee at the time, so there's no statue of Claudette at the capitol. She was a nurse's aide and probably told her story and people were like, "That's messed up," but then they told some other story about how they could've played for the White Sox but they were sick the day of the tryouts or whatever and she had to act like that was the same thing. Meanwhile she's thinking, "Hey, asshole, my thing actually happened!!! I would've been famous and sparked a movement." But anyway, I guess it happened the way it happened and that's it.

Huntsville, Alabama, is where the first space rocket was launched by Wernher von Braun, an ex-Nazi that we brought over after the war. He apparently did a lot of good work for the United States, although I'm sure there were a couple of awkward nights when he was reminiscing after a few too many drinks about "the good old days." I feel like Alabama is a state that epitomizes how different people in this country are. I mean, they've got Mississippi on one side of them—the

Randy Quaid family to their Griswolds. And then they've got Florida on the other side, which is the state whose state sign says "Welcome to Florida! Excuse the place, I didn't get a chance to clean up from last night."

Alabama is the South and they won't ever not be. They like church and they hate abortion. And everybody says you have to evolve, but if evolution means being like the North, Alabama will probably look and say the North got its own problems. It's hard to take advice from any state because none of 'em seem to be doing it well enough to be ordering any of the others around. So unless we set up some mandatory American group-therapy conventions every year or so, nobody is going to change. It's too anti–Tenth Amendment to tell people to change their culture unless there's a great reason for it. Segregation was a great reason. Abortion is a lot more arguable. But there will never be a constitutional convention again because it's too complicated, and it's never going to be perfect. Because nothing's perfect, except that fifty-yard spiral that the kid from Muscle Shoals threw last week against Mobile Central.

★ ★ ★

ARKANSAS

BIG-BOX STATE

You almost made it big in the late 90s, Arkansas. You had Bill Clinton and Billy Bob Thornton, and the Razorbacks made the Final Four a few times! But you petered out. Oh, well. I could say the same thing about my career during that decade. The state that pronounces it different from Kansas. What is your problem? Are you looking for attention? So that's strike 1. It's actually against the law to not pronounce it the French way in Arkansas. I guess there's not a lot of people doing time for mispronunciation. But what do I know? If they want to be fancy once in a while, they have the right: Arkansas has a diamond mine open to the public, and a thirteen-year-old girl found a 2.93 carat diamond. Can you imagine some guy decides to buy her an engagement ring? He shows her the ring, asks her to marry him. She says, "What's this cheap piece of shit?"

Hot Springs, Arkansas, was the neutral ground for the mafia for some reason. Back in the day, the made men would go there and it would be a ceasefire. Nobody is sure why they picked it. Maybe because it reminded them of the Roman baths and they always wanted to be like the

Romans? But Arkansas is just one of those states where, when people name all the places down South, then they go, "Oh yeah, and Arkansas." Forgettable is not a way to go. When Clinton was president, it was kind of the first time people gave you a little bit of respect. But the minute he left, it was back to the wave across the room as we're passing by on the way to Texas or somewhere.

Paul McCartney says *Blackbird* was inspired by the desegregation in Little Rock in 1957. And Charles Manson even had his demons write the word "Arise" on the walls in blood at the murder scenes. So I guess that means Manson's interpretation of *The White Album* as a prelude to race war was true. I guess he wasn't so crazy after all, was he? I'm not going to go so far as to say we owe Charles Manson an apology . . . but yes, we do. I'm going on record with that. Another strange thing about Arkansas is the Dover lights, which are a mysterious phenomenon over in the Ozarks. The legend says it's Spanish conquistador ghosts looking for their lost treasure. Plus, there's a Bigfoot type who runs around known as the Boggy Creek Monster. He kills cattle and dogs. You've got some weird Resident Evil–type stuff going on down there, huh?

Thank God for Walmart. I mean, they keep you relevant in a way. People reference Walmart all the time. Not always in a positive way, but nobody can deny that Walmart literally changed the game. Because they said, "Not only can you come in on a mobile scooter, we will have somebody say hello to you. Not only can you wear your underwear or pajamas to shop, but we accept you." And everybody wants acceptance. And ol' Sam Walton understood that. Nobody wants to be judged on their twenty-year-old tramp stamp as they lean over to slap their eight-year-old daughter who's wearing a shirt that says JAILBAIT. I guarantee one thing. The most hated man in the history of Arkansas is Jeff Bezos. He better never set foot in that state because he's the number one Walmart killer. He took Walmart and put it online. And now you can stay at home and shop! And now you don't even have to wear underwear while you're doing it.

Arkansas was originally part of the Louisiana Purchase, and from what I understand America was forced to take Arkansas as part of the package or France wouldn't do the deal. The Louisiana Purchase was one of those deals where two countries are negotiating over land and all the Indian tribes are sitting there the whole time and they don't even realize what's happening. And we got it cheap because we bought so much. So it was that philosophy that probably inspired Walmart. Somewhere in the DNA of Arkansans are the strands that led to Sam Walton. The Louisiana Purchase was $15 million for fifteen states. It was the first bulk purchase by America.

FLORIDA

A HOT MESS

You are such a great symbol of all the diversity and contradictory nature of America. You are the beautiful beach and the pungent meth lab. You are the skinny model in South Beach and the fat warehouse worker in Jacksonville. You're the Jews and Cubans down south and white and black rednecks up north. And in between you've got millions of people who have a look in their eyes like they just served two tours of duty because there are a lot of normal people in Florida and they don't like to leave their houses. Florida was Seminole Indians and a Spanish colony. But then Georgia and South Carolina settlers started moving in because Spain didn't have enough troops to control the North and the people known as "Florida crackers" were the first to introduce the term until the word "redneck" replaced it in 1900. And so Spain gave Florida up. And Andrew Jackson came in and conquered the Seminoles. And the United States had another coastal state. John Quincy Adams described Florida along the lines of a "derelict that serves no other purpose than as a post to the United States." Which I think is a description even Floridians would agree with.

When people say "Florida," they always think of South Florida first, of course. Miami primarily. That Jewish/Cuban/Haitian tourism board that has to deal with every generation's hedonists and hustlers from Brazil to Russia and all of the United States. Miami is all the people who want to live the American dream first. By which I mean most people work hard for thirty years and save enough money to finally get enough to buy a little place in the sun for retirement. Now Miami is all the party animals from all over the country and world who say, "I'm not going to work for thirty years; I'll skip that step and go right to the place in the sun. I'll get a job down there DJ'ing or dealing drugs or, ideally, both." And the whole skyline was built by cocaine money. It's amazing what kind of enterprise money laundering can be responsible for. We all talk about the bad side of drug dealers, but when you're on your balcony on the 45th floor overlooking Biscayne Bay, maybe you should say a quick prayer to the Medellín cartel.

Then you have Daytona, which is the gold coast for the outlaw bikers and the women who love them. I lived there once in '79 and worked in a T-shirt store. So Daytona was quite a fun time going to the beach and so on, but the place I lived was sketchy, to put it mildly. Half the businesses were drug and prostitution rings and the other half were criminals on the run. One night a biker knocked on my door in just his tighty whiteys and threatened to carve my face up if I didn't pay him for some under-the-counter medications I had purchased, and I had to explain to him the payroll schedule of small businesses like Wild N Crazy T-shirts. That was a little dicey. And then there was the soda machine incident, where a runaway/hooker and I got into an extended conversation about Van Halen because "Dance the Night Away" was the song of the summer and I thought we'd hit it off. So later I knocked on her door to take the romance to the next level, and she told me to get the fuck away from her, she was doing business. I returned to Daytona years later in triumph during my MTV days and never saw the old crowd, although I hope a couple of them looked out their windows and gave the begrudging slow clap like, "Good for you, one of us made it."

Then there's the west coast of Florida. Tampa, St. Pete, etc. Even the west coast people are nuts. You'd think that the Gulf Coast would be the peaceful coast, but nope. They are as sick as the other one. It's not that they are criminal, it's just that they are not respectable for the most part. That's why it's better to just go there for vacations. Because something will happen by the end of the week that will just make you go, "Start the car." Orlando is Orlando. It's Disney for about thirty blocks and then it's Compton in 1985 for the next ten miles.

There are a few other parts of Florida worth mentioning. Coral Castle in Homestead. You probably never heard of it. This guy Ed Leedskalnin who was just over 5 feet tall and 100 pounds built an entire stone castle and garden with thousands of pounds of rocks. No one ever witnessed him moving these 60,000-pound stones with no help and no equipment and this was back in the 1920s thru the 40s. Ed would only say he knew the secrets of the pyramids and you could too. But nobody has ever figured it out. I wish I could. I wouldn't use it to build a stone castle. I would use it to challenge any champion MMA fighter to a fight and then fling them around the ring with my pinky finger. Tell me that's not every man's dream. Then you walk over to a football field and you challenge the whole team against just you. You run them down and score at will.

Cocoa Beach/Cape Canaveral are both very respectable and then there's all these cool places like Cassadaga, where they are all psychics. I always planned on going there but never made it. I feel like maybe that town is responsible for Florida's madness. They probably all got bored from having no variety, so they decided to put a curse on the whole state. One night they decided, "We are going to put a hex on the whole place and make everybody just a little bit off. Not noticeable in a big way but just small enough where it has a butterfly effect, and in twenty years it'll be a car wreck." And that's what went down.

You are famous for having the most golf courses, which is a sign of an aging population, to put it mildly. You already had the people dressed for it, so the easy part was mowing the grass. You are also famous for taking some of the heat off New Jersey because all state jokes used to be about New Jersey and now half the jokes are about Florida. You are famous for *Scarface,* which is the ultimate Florida movie: you move in, you get rich, and you dress and act like an asshole until you die.

But I still love Florida. You stand alone. Because you are unique and because we don't want to stand too close to you because we might get arrested too. Florida does the job as the vacation party state. You're the wild kid on the block that we're not allowed to hang out with. But sometimes we just want to break the rules.

★ ★ ★

WEST VIRGINIA

COLLECTIVE UNCONSCIOUS

I don't know why I have them in the Southern section. They are not really the South. They are also not really the Midwest. West Virginia's always been on their own. They seceded from Virginia because of the Civil War. Pretty wild. It is the only state to break up. Chicago tried to break up with Illinois a bunch of times, but the rest of the state kept giving them more legislative power because they felt the population blah blah—you know the argument. It's the same argument around the Electoral College. But Illinois gave it up, so Chicago stayed. But if shady Chicago politicians in the 1920s couldn't finagle a bunch of farmers, they would've been kicked out of the ward. West Kansas tried to leave in 1992 because they felt those slick big-city boys in Topeka were taking advantage of them. Alaska, Maine . . . a lot of places have threatened to secede, but West Virginia was the only one that did it.

They have always gone against everybody. Mountain people are shady. Or maybe mountains make people shady. It's physical and becomes psychological. Geography breeds personality. And when you are up there in the mountains looking down at the valley, you start to get weird. You see the people like they are ants or something. Like the observer effect. It changes what you observe, but it also changes the observer. Mountain people are used to spending a lot of time looking at other people from a distance and the people turn into lab rats to them. And then when they look up and catch you looking, you start to feel guilty and you hide behind a tree or something and suddenly you are becoming secretive and strange. And you don't even know what you are hiding for; you're allowed to look at people. You are on your property. But you start becoming weird.

They were also the moonshiners. Making white lightning was a big business back before the Revolutionary War and right after. When Congress decided to tax it, the mountain people all exploded and you had the Whiskey Rebellion and George Washington himself had to lead the troops and crush the rebellion. You know how rebellious you have to be to be part of America and start a war with George fucking Washington? That's almost admirable, the balls it takes. They finally gave up on the idea, but it was real foreshadowing of the conflict of state vs. federal authority that was going to be a problem for everybody in this country from then all the way through till today. You can't tell mountain people how to live when you are on the plains and vice versa.

And there's the incest jokes. For whatever combination of reasons, it's a stereotype about a few southern states, but West Virginia the most. And stereotypes as we all know are generalizations and generalizations are not true. Well, they have elements of truth—that's why they came about in the first place. I'm sure that there was a lot of it going on, but you have to realize that it happened throughout history. Everyone's living miles apart so you don't have access to a lot of other potential romantic partners and then you take out the percentage of attractive people, and there were no dating apps. I'm not defending incest. I mean, I am, but I'm just trying to look at it from their point of view. You have a high infant-mortality rate and the average person dies of black lung at thirty-two and your hot cousin comes to visit and you think, "What am I doing? Life is short!" Because we all have had hot relatives that we were attracted to. Maybe those West Virginia coal mines represent the part of our unconscious that wants to explore dark tunnels. The id of our country.

★ ★ ★

THE MIDWEST

A man who works hard stinks only to the ones that have
nothing to do but smell.
—LAURA INGALLS WILDER

Although now they're known for friendly moms delivering baked goods, their forbearers (the early settlers) had to be ready to die and to kill. There was nobody to help you if your family had a problem. No government, no laws. What do you do if the left flank of a 58,000-head buffalo herd plows through the side of your log cabin? What are you gonna do, call 911? You had to handle it on your own. If you lost your coat in winter, you had to kill something and climb inside its body to keep warm. Do you know what kind of person you have to become to be capable of doing that?

We came in hot, no doubt. We were on the warpath. There was all that land, and it wasn't said out loud but it was implied that if you wanted some of it, you'd probably have a little interaction with the in-digenous people. And it would probably end in violence. You were your own lawyer, doctor, real estate agent. All on your own: a gun was your insurance policy if somebody borrowed something from you and didn't return it. It was also the lawyer that negotiated for you if someone came on your property. An ax was your real estate agent and your shopping cart. The Bible was your iPad. You would binge read Leviticus. The animals were your supermarket. You went shopping with a knife. Rubbing two sticks together to make a campfire was your utilities. You see the bill this month? How many sticks are you using?? Staking a claim was your lease. You could own it, but the lease was there because you had to worry about getting murdered by animals. Killed by a bear. The health care system was this: they'd lay you in a bag of leaves, give you a stick to bite, and then saw off the infected limb. Then they'd give you the stick you'd been biting on as a crutch and tell you to walk it off.

In the old days you had nothing. No Band-Aids, no tampons, no soap to wash with. You just smelled all the time. No combs to control your hair, no spare tools. You just found things in nature and then sliced them with your knife until they were shaped like a tool.

But in that environment people got used to individual rights. They got used to freedom out there in the Midwest. Even more freedom than the East Coast. The East Coast was all immigrants, so a little freedom felt like a lot. The Midwest was immigrants *and* some second generation. So they weren't satisfied with eight kids sleeping in a tenement; they wanted their "own bedroom."

★ ★ ★

OHIO

THE GUINEA PIG STATE

Ohio is part of the Northwest Territory from the Treaty of Paris. The first frontier. The first chance for the government to put the system we created into action. The first new states. Ohio. And Ohioans took it seriously. They didn't play around with slavery or greed. They were earnest people. You needed canal-building OCD Germans. That's what Ohio had; it wasn't a state that seemed like it had a lot of resources to get rich, so you had to really want to be just a hardworking farmer. If you got injured, you had nothing coming and that's what you got. And they are still like that. Always in the middle. Half the state has that Kentucky accent, the other half has that Great Lakes accent. They had the auto plants and the steel plants, but were never Detroit or Pittsburgh. Always the middle child. The good middle child.

Land is what the American dream was. To own land meant something. Because throughout history all the landowners had been lords, dukes, earls, viscounts. All the rich, powerful, and connected. And now you could be a little bit like them. And that's what America promised.

You could be like those people. Without royal bloodlines, without connections, without titles. With just hard work. And so all the hard workers went out there, and there was always a good character in the old movies who would say, "I'm not afraid of hard work." And you knew that character was from Midwestern farmer stock. But he'd be the one to get killed. Because along with the hard workers, there was another group that would always come out: thieves. They got chased out of wherever they were from back east and decided to come out where you could rob and cheat and kill without government intervention.

Sincerity took Ohio a long way. It was the state everybody liked. The state that did moderation right. Because Cleveland was made up of all the early-twentieth-century Eastern Europeans. Hungarians, Serbs, who came over here right before World War I. Which started when the Serbs killed that Archduke Franz Ferdinand. They probably figured nobody would get that mad if they killed an archduke. They probably figured it's not like killing a duke. It's an archduke. But for some reason, that set it off and they've been paying the price ever since. Except the ones who made it to Ohio.

Ohio has all these cities that are just art installations of ten blocks of rusted steel carcasses. Nothing more depressing than a bad city in Ohio. Because it's just too symbolic of the fall of the country and Ohio doesn't deserve that fate because they're hardworking but not Puritan, religious but not Calvinist, football fans but not fanatics—Ohio is the example of how the country was supposed to behave. And where did it get them? It got them a front seat on the train to meh.

Nobody thinks about Ohio hatefully or lovingly. We just assume they will be there when we need them, like your aunt who always gives you a birthday card with twenty bucks. You don't treat her nice and you don't think about her, but if that twenty bucks isn't there, you go apeshit. The problem with Ohio is that people take Ohio for granted. Because Ohio allows it. And yet there's something hopeful about Ohio. Innocent and hopeful. And Columbus and Cincinnati are the hot spots now. It used to be Cleveland and Akron. How did Akron lose clout? When they went radial tire? It seemed like the right move at the time. And even when they were booming with rubber and steel and coal, Ohio never really changed. They never got conceited. That's Ohio.

They're the state that everybody watches during the election season. As Ohio goes, so goes the nation. Basically, it's the place all the candidates have to win to win the presidency.

So, they all kiss Ohio's ass for the months leading up to every election. And Ohio falls for it every four years, don't you? They come in smiling, shaking hands, promising jobs, and you are like the battered wife. "This time he means it." "I can see he's changed." And then the elections are over and you're sitting there with Cleveland and Akron and Springfield and Dayton picking themselves up off the floor and saying, "I fell. I'm so clumsy. It's my fault." Because you're too nice to use that six months of power effectively. If I were Ohio, I would make every presidential candidate sign a pact that if they didn't deliver one million jobs to Ohio the first year, they would have to cut off their ear. And post it on Instagram. And every year after that, the same thing. Or haze the candidates. Make them strip to their underwear during the debate. These are just ideas. To get you to know what it feels like to be in power. And to liven things up. Sometimes you need an outsider to see yourself the way you really are.

Ohio is the normal state. They are not too liberal, not too conservative. Everybody else is out there drinking and screaming and fighting and they just fold their laundry. That's what their motto should say as you enter the state: "Welcome to Ohio. The way it was supposed to be."

★ ★ ★

INDIANA

THIRTY-FOOT JUMPER AND THOUSAND-YARD STARE

You drive through Indiana and there's a basketball hoop attached to every garage and there's somebody shooting around. I love Indiana because it's one of those states that cares only about basketball. Even though it has a lot of farmers. They play basketball in overalls. When you think of Indiana basketball, you think of vintage Bobby Knight from the 80s. The angriest coach in history. He looked and acted like what Trump would look and act like as a coach. He never smiled. He kicked his players and threw chairs. He had anger issues. But nobody ever said, "Hey, Coach! You have an abusive childhood?" Because people didn't talk that way in those days. The announcers didn't say, "Wow! Coach Knight is really misplacing his anger today, boy! Oh man, the coach is screaming at the refs like his father screamed at him back on the farm. I'll be honest with you, Charles—I've never seen a clearer picture of the damaged child that is one of the winningest coaches in the Midwest Conference than we are seeing here today." "You said it, Brett. This guy is a textbook example of a cycle of abuse." But Knight had some good qualities compared with other coaches. He wasn't a sexual abuser, at least, and he made all his players go to class. Those are the two choices you have in life: either you can go with a verbally abusive bastard who plays by the rules or a secret sexual deviant whom the players like but who's getting millions from Nike. Which one are you? Which one am I? Most of us probably think, "I'd be the player," because everybody always sees themselves as the victim/hero. Like when people ask whether you would be a good German who goes along with the Nazis or a resister? Nobody is ever the Nazi. Well, guess what? There were a lot of Nazis back then. They had to be somebody's baby, as Jackson Browne would say. I don't think he was writing that song about Nazis, by the way. But you never know. Alert: I just googled Jackson Browne at this moment, and guess where he was born? Heidelberg, Germany!! Call it providence, call it coincidence, but that was one I will always cherish. "Somebody's Baby" was probably written about Josef Mengele.

But the real king of Indiana is JCM. John Cougar Mellencamp. This guy put in work. What's more Indiana than "Jack and Diane"? munching on chili dogs outside the Tastee Freeze. "Pink Houses." Another masterpiece of Indiana. I remember I hated Mellencamp when he started because I was watching his video with a girl on my lap and she said, "Hey, he's cute." She didn't have to say it out loud. Most girls just give each other a look when they see someone cute and they're sitting on a guy's lap. But not this girl. She just had to blurt it out. "Hey, he's cute!" I don't know what her problem was, but it still pisses me off—although less so than at the time. And I know some of you people are saying, "If you were really secure, you wouldn't be threatened by that kind of comment." Um. Duh. Yeah, no shit. If I were really secure, I wouldn't have destroyed and sabotaged fifteen golden opportunities and I'd be dictating this book to a lowly group of assistants on a beach in Spain. But that's not the way life plays out. Look at your life. Are you secure? I thought so. There's two sides to this. Don't open up a can of worms! Speaking of horrible expressions. Can of worms?? That's a little strange. Is that an old fishing-hole expression? Where would you find a can of worms? Other than in a John Cougar Mellencamp song? "Sitting at the fishin' hole, a bag of canned wo-orms!! Small-town boy all day and night, as far as that's concerned!!" I'm not a songwriter but I like to believe I could be, in a kind of Eugene Landy way.

Indiana is one of those corn states. Corn itself is a weird crop because it's mostly for other farmers for their livestock. Corn farmers are the comedians' comedians of farmers. We don't get corn farmers, but the other farmers probably stop their trucks in the middle of the road and watch them work in the field for a half hour and go, "People are so stupid, how could they not appreciate this, don't they see this guy is a genius?"

I guess the point is that Indiana is hard to figure out. There's a hoop in every driveway next to a tractor. It's strange—you'd think they'd like football or baseball because they spend all that time in fields. But maybe that's actually it. They're so sick of being in the fields that they don't want to see a field when they're relaxing. And in hockey the ice reminds them of the destruction of their crops, so that leaves basketball. God bless you, Indiana. You're the reason they invented a three-point line.

Indianans don't blink. I don't know why. But it probably has something to do with looking out over the fields. Probably trying to spot any kind of infestations or deformities in the crops. Indiana is one of those states where people are all about the honor system. If you steal something, they can't even believe it. Because they don't want anything free. Ever. They represent that part of our country. The states that think anybody who gets any government benefits is a freeloader. They've been quietly stewing over it since the New Deal, but they'll never say anything because they're Indianans. They just stare.

★★★
ILLINOIS
NEW YORK FOR XL PEOPLE

Chicago and . . . okay, we are fine with just Chicago. The New York for friendly people. Fat necks and slaughterhouses. You put an animal in front of them, they instinctively pick up a boning knife and start swinging. It just sets them off like Leatherface from *The Texas Chainsaw Massacre* when an unwanted guest shows up. They put on the apron and start waving around a cleaver. But it's the blocked heart and soul of the Midwest. And even though Chicago's a big city, they still have that Midwest accent and attitude. They are sort of rough-and-tumble, but still backslapping friendly. And everybody eats red meat. Cardiologists have removed fully cooked steaks from people's chests.

The rest of Illinois are farmers. People don't realize the state is 80 percent farmland. You don't think about it because nobody leaves Chicago, but the rest of it is really the great farms. It is funny how much of the world is farms and farmers. Big agriculture is the bad guy today, but at this point we shouldn't kid ourselves that the small farmer is going to have any power against multinationals that have taken over the farms.

Things don't go backward unless there's a catastrophe. And even catastrophes likely will lead to more regulation from the corporations. The multinationals who have bought the small family farms are probably forcing farmers to have corporate culture. Meetings where they tell a bunch of guys in overalls how to manage expectations and encourage innovation and have team-building exercises for the chickens. They send managers around to motivate the farmers. They have to put up quotes around the farm: "Always be harvesting." "Make a goal an opportunity." HR tells them you can no longer milk the cow without verbal consent.

Cargill. Monsanto. Archer Daniels Midland. It started so simply. A few farmers got together to form collectives to protect against rustlers. Then one of their kids was a nerd who went to college and came up with "efficiency" and now look: biofuels. Concentrated Animal Feeding Operations where they've got animals living up against each other like UCB students in a Bushwick railroad flat. We've dead zoned the Gulf of Mexico with chemical runoff from fertilizer, so if you are a plankton you probably have twelve lawsuits going on right now. And they bring up all the Mexicans to work in the slaughterhouses because the Americans don't want to do that work for six bucks an hour. All the slaughterhouses used to be in the Chicago streets. They got all these Polish and Slavic immigrants to come over and work twenty hours a day for three cents and whatever you could chew off the sides of beef while you were carrying them around the factory floor. Then in the twentieth century Chicago became the city to move to for the breadbasket kids. Everybody else has a couple of skyscrapers and a couple of subway stations, but they're not moving millions of people a day back and forth. That's the job of a city. Bring people in every morning and ship them back out every night. And only New York and Chicago have enough personality where people say, "You don't have to ship me out. I'm going to live here." Let's face it, those are the big boys of cities.

Illinois is still humble compared with New York, but they can get cocky. It's called the Land of Lincoln, but Lincoln was from Kentucky.

He moved to Illinois when he was about twenty, and they have the balls to claim him while Kentucky just sits quiet. But that's a good life lesson: if you let other people walk all over you, they will. That's for sure. And Kentucky should just change their license plate to "Home of Lincoln." Or "Original Lincoln" if they want to give Illinois a little bit of shit.

But Illinois is the capital of the Midwest. Now they use those fat wrists and fat fingers that used to rip sides of cattle into steaks to put people from the rest of the Midwest in bro hugs and say, "Welcome. You don't need New York or LA. We are city enough, we got you."

★ ★ ★

MISSOURI

HIGHWAY TO HELL

T. S. Eliot saw a wasteland
Spread out against the sky
Burt Bacharach grew up there
But he chose to walk on by

It's almost impossible to understand Missouri. It's a Southern state but it's also a Midwestern state. It's got the St. Louis Arch and nobody really understands why that's even a thing. It was built as a monument to "westward expansion," so I'm surprised it hasn't been torn down yet or renamed the gateway to genocide. It's where Lewis and Clark made their move to explore the West. Thomas Jefferson sent them: it wasn't like they decided to do it on their own. They were just "doing their job," as the saying goes. It's all ex-Germans in St. Louis so people got it. By the way, that had to be an awkward time for St. Louis and Missouri during World War II. We were fighting the Nazis and Herr Anheuser-Busch are selling Budweiser all over the country. This giant German word on every can and bottle and glass. In German I think "Budweiser" means "foot soldier." The point is that Eberhard Anheuser and Augustus Busch formed an unholy alliance in the 1850s and dominated the industry—as Germans tend to do. But during World War II, I'm sure they had to tell their workers "keep ze radio down" when they were listening to the war news and cheering the early victories like the Luftwaffe were the 2004 Cardinals. St. Louis loves baseball even though they are not that great at it. Because beer and pretzels and hot dogs and sauerkraut probably make them feel like they are back in the old country. All they need is a pair of overall jorts and an uneven fedora and they are, Achtung, baby. I kid Germany, but don't forget that without them the Beatles would've been a bar band in northern England with a couple of Chuck Berry covers and no teeth. Chuck Berry is also from Missouri, and ragtime, which nobody enjoys; and Branson. Which is the family-friendly entertainment capital of the world. It's kind of a Christian Vegas. Branson has Dolly Parton's Stampede, where you watch a bunch of two-show-a-day alcoholic buffalo stumble around like Judy Garland at the London Palladium.

Then you can visit the historic home of Mark Twain, where they do readings of a redacted version of *Huckleberry Finn*. That's the problem with historical sites and history in general. There's a lot of "triggering" going on, so people are trying to eliminate it. I believe nobody born before the twentieth century should be held responsible for anything they did because everybody was a savage until electricity, which was around 1880-something. It was literally and figuratively the Dark Ages until then. People act like America is the only place that was founded on bloodshed and exploitation. Every place on this planet that has a building was built on some hut that was once the dwelling of a smaller tribe until the bigger tribe showed up and said, "How come they have a view of the lake and we are stuck next to that rockslide?" And then they made it happen. That's what the Pilgrims did and that's what the Romans did and everybody in history did. Large and small. From Genghis Khan to Columbus to the real estate developer that builds a high-rise in front of your house so your view—which used to be one that allowed you to open the window, and look all the way down to the river and the bridge—now only allows you to wave at a doughy software engineer on a Peloton. But in our age people are trying to rectify all historical injustice. The past was filled with power players, greedy sociopaths, scheming scoundrels, and dastardly fucks. And the "age of discovery"—a presumptuous phrase for invading a place that people already lived in—will never feel okay because you can't change the past. And people never forgive anyway. We've all had people we haven't seen since we were kids come up to us at bars or reunions or family picnics and say, "You pushed me off the swings when we were seven" or "You cut in front of me at the ice cream truck." So, there's no forgiveness on a grand scale, only revenge. I'm sorry to sound like an eighty-year-old Bulgarian peasant woman who's lived through six wars, but this is how I think it goes.

The point is that every landmark and historical site has a few bloodstains on it if you look closely. And so, Missouri's Gateway Arch is a gateway to freedom and opportunity for some and a circle of hell to others.

MICHIGAN

THE LION IN WINTER

Michigan is the Midwest but with more of a personality. The quiet states like to talk because they are used to being alone. There was a famous French general explorer named Cadillac who built the fort that became Detroit, and whoever had Fort Detroit had the Midwest. The French had it, then the British, and then us after the Revolutionary War. Then when the Erie Canal opened, a lot of New England people who wanted their own farms went out to Michigan, because there wasn't enough land in New England. You could've fooled me if you've ever been to New England.

But obviously Henry Ford is Michigan, for better or for worse. He changed the game. Henry Ford was to cars what St. Paul was to Christians: he didn't invent them, but before him there were only, like, seven in the whole world. His assembly-line concept and mass industrialization made the twentieth century, which made this country. Ford made Detroit the capital of cars, and cars are the most American thing in the world. We've always loved cars. A car is a real place where you feel real freedom.

When you are by yourself in your car, you relax, reflect, plot, curse, cry, and sing. Car culture is the perfect reflection of a society of individuals. Your car is who you are. You're in traffic, surrounded, yet by yourself. You pull up in your car. Pulling up is as important as driving. Because if you have a nice car, people pause for a moment and say, "Whose car is that?" And when you get out, all eyes are on you. And on the other hand, if you're parked somewhere and don't have a nice car, you know people are going, "Whose shitbox is this?" And COVID-19 has made our cars even more important. They're our safe rooms on wheels. Henry Ford was the inventor of the forty-hour workweek, doubling wages, and creating profit sharing for workers. He also was at the forefront of hiring goons to beat union organizers and put out his own anti-Semitic periodicals. He died like a rat in 1947. He was a bad guy and a great guy, and he was the twentieth century.

Unions became big because of the car industry, and the whole thing started in Detroit. It was this revolutionary place. It shook the world.

Henry Ford and his mechanization really made people pay attention to labor. Jimmy Hoffa started organizing in Detroit: the Teamsters Local 299. No one had ever seen working people with self-esteem before America. Before America, working people took abuse and felt like they deserved it. But Hoffa gave the average truck driver a little bit of self-worth. And that's why they loved him. Unfortunately, the robber barons hired goons whom Hoffa had to make deals with or they would've killed him. But the goons switched sides and took over the union, and you get the last Scorsese movie. But it was an amazing run. And today people say, "The jobs Americans won't do" as if that's a bad thing. That's what it's been all about for the past seventy-five years. Part of the American contract that we all made was that you didn't work till you dropped dead. You had benefits and vacations and you didn't work 100 percent. You agreed to certain standards of productivity and it was a nice balance. That's why you have three generations of union workers. When did it stop working? Everybody has a theory. The greed of the corporations, the power of investors, or the corruption of union officials. And then one executive said at a board meeting, "I know some people who will work for half of what you're paying. Only problem is, they live about 1,800 miles south of the factory."

Detroit has been trying to make a comeback since the riots of 1967 and the Japanese and German auto boom of the 1970s, and it's just never happened. I see the whole thing as another microcosm of America. The greatest and yet most violent and brutal; the fairest and most lucrative, equal, and hardworking; the greediest and yet the most generous. And racial divisions and then pride and the fall and now just a husk. And obviously Detroit is not the only place like that. A lot of the Rust Belt fell for various reasons. But Detroit was the first, the biggest and the best America's City. And now no one even thinks about it unless you're surfing through the channels and *8 Mile* is on.

IOWA

CAULIFLOWERED EARS OF CORN

They have the whitest hair in America. Even whiter than Indiana. Was it the Germans? Or the Dutch? There are a lot of Van Somethings out there. Which is Dutch. And Von is German. And a lot of Germanic surnames. I'm not talking about Florida-white hair like when you get old. I'm talking about the white hair that you won't see outside the most northern parts of Sweden. If you looked at the Iowa State Fair from a plane in 1972, it probably looked like a cotton field. Hogs outnumber humans 4 to 1 in Iowa. Which sounds pretty funny except when you think about it, rats probably are in the same proportion to people in New York City.

It's where Buddy Holly and Ritchie Valens and the Big Bopper died in that plane crash. And Waylon Jennings made a joke at the Big Bopper when the Big Bopper said the bus would be freezing: "I hope your plane crashes." Wow. Then when it crashed, he said for years that he felt as if he'd caused it. I wonder what made him stop feeling like he caused it. Because I still think he caused it.

Iowa is another of those states where they don't believe in running their mouth all the time. They keep it relatively quiet and they look suspiciously at people that are always putting their two cents in. A lot of these Midwestern states are mistrustful of glib people, because the only glib people they came into contact with for hundreds of years were the peddlers and the snake oil salesmen that came through town. Opinions are never practical. Like if you were working the farm and someone said, "I don't think we are going to have an early harvest," that was just an opinion. And if it turned out to be wrong and you starved to death, then it was your fault for listening to an opinion. It wasn't about speculation. That was for the big-city boys over in Chicago or the bankers in New York and Philadelphia. (Do you believe there was a time when those Philly dirtbags were considered elitist and snobby?) So Iowans don't like to jabber on, as they probably call it.

Iowa is known to have the highest literacy rate in the nation. That's because when the nearest person is a hundred miles away, there's nothing to do but read. Before the cell phone, you couldn't text. You had to walk ten miles to the nearest phone, and then everybody in town knew who you were calling. And the word spread: Betsy Heinrech was talking to little Tommy Muller; they had a couple of conversations of more than seven minutes this week. If you spoke more than seven minutes, you were engaged. There were no booty calls. No kid ever went to the ice cream parlor and got on the pay phone and went through the operator to have her say, "I have a person-to-person call from little Timmy Scheigonhoffer, he wants to know if you up?" The phone operator had all the power. She was the first person the cops went to when there was a crime. Although there was only a crime once a year. Usually involving the theft of some kind of farming equipment. When I think of Iowa, I think of farming and wrestling. Because, for whatever combination of reasons, Iowa is the wrestling capital of the world. And if you try to argue that, you will find yourself in a fireman's carry followed by an illegal body slam to the mat. There's a guy named Dan Gable, who is the king of Iowa. He's a true champion of a man. He beat the Soviets in the '72

Olympics without giving up one point. Their only goal was to defeat Dan Gable. When you are talked about in the Soviet Union at high-level meetings in the Kremlin in 1972 because of your wrestling, that's pretty impressive. But wrestling is also a clean sport. Iowa has a lot of those pork processing plants, so when you spend your day surrounded by flying pork pieces and bloody aprons and beheaded pigs, you want to see a sport on a nice mat that's still manly but not messy and bloodstained.

I don't want you to think that Iowa is a bunch of quiet hog-slaughtering wrestlers but if they are, there's a lot worse things to be. They keep their mouths shut and they aren't afraid to get a little blood on their hands. And the wrestling thing sounds strange, but it's because they were German and farmers and Midwesterners, so they had to figure out how to have physical contact without being soft. It's their way of expressing to another man, "Hey, I really care about you and I'm glad to see you." They are not emotional people. A backslap is considered intimate. A married couple will bump fists or maybe give each other a high five on their anniversary. Iowa is no-frills. They think emotions are indulgent. They are the last of that old-school "I show you my love by going to work every day and coming home right after" America.

I was in Iowa a few times, and one of those times in the 90s I'm staying at a small Motel 6–type place (when you do colleges, there aren't any diva hotels like I usually stay in). But anyway, I wanted to do laundry and one of the cleaning ladies who looked like she'd had to deal with a lifetime of hard luck was in there. And she said, "I'll do it." So, I said, "Thanks." Then I came back and it was all done and folded and I said, "Thanks," and went to hand her fifty bucks. And she said, "No thanks." And I said, "Please." And she said, "No thank you" and I said, "I'm leaving it here." And she said, "No, sir. I was doing it anyway." And I tried to convince her to take the money for ten minutes, and she finally just left. I know it's not everybody, but that's a certain type of Midwesterner that thinks taking a tip when you're doing the work anyway is freeloading. And if there's one thing Iowans hate in the fields and the laundry room is a parasite.

WISCONSIN

THE DIET STARTS TOMORROW

I don't want to fat shame, but I heard the state bird is an original-recipe eagle. I've been going to Wisconsin since the late 80s and I have to say, they really had that fat-hipster-who's-good-with-electrical-and-plumbing thing down even back then. They actually invented the neckbeard, which a lot of people don't know and even fewer people care about. Bratwurst. Beer. All the restaurants look like a VFW hall.

Wisconsin people are friendly. I think they have a thing with Minnesota, but that's every state. Every state has a problem with the state next to it. That's just the way human nature is. Whoever is near you, you hate. Texas? Oklahoma. New York? New Jersey. That's why Alaska and Hawaii never really fit in as states. They don't have anybody next to them. Alaska has the North Pole and Hawaii has the Pacific Ocean. How do you make fun of an ocean? Talk about how salty it is? Or how it's not salty enough? Besides, everybody loves the ocean. It's like making fun of a baby. The Hawaiian Islands can make fun of each other, I guess. Hey, how about the Big Island? Or something like that. But we're not talking about Hawaiians right now—this is about Wisconsin. The fatsos. Not that Hawaiians aren't fat themselves. In fact, I've never seen a thin Hawaiian. Or a thin Wisconsinite. They wear it well, though. When you look at them, they fit their fat correctly. It looks good on them. Their hands are proportionate to their fat. They have thick fingers and fat hands.

But back to the mighty cheese state. There's something about people that make cheese that bugs me big-time. I don't like it when people eat cheese. Just the way they bite down in slow motion makes me angry and sick. Because I don't really like cheese myself. Except for on pizza. Their bratwurst is fine, though. Beer and bratwurst are what they love in Wisconsin. Yeah, it's the Nazi diet. That's how Hitler got popular. He'd walk into the beer halls and start glad-handing everybody. "Hey, how you doing? How's the beer, Hans? Hey, Rolf, you are really killing that bratwurst!" I'm not saying Wisconsinites are Nazis. But I am saying Nazis would feel happier in Wisconsin than, say, in New Mexico. Because of all the Mexicans. Although to be fair, the Nazis never really weighed in on Latin people. They had plenty to say about the Jews and they even got racial about black people with Jesse Owens but they partnered with Japan, so you can't say they were totally racist. And on Mexicans Hitler never gave a speech, "Und vee must stop zees Mexicans auf augen shvienhunt!" I'm not trying to be a Nazi apologist. I don't doubt that Hitler would've been the same no matter where he was. Hitler gonna be Hitler. But maybe for geographic reasons. Like I said, whoever's next to you. He hated Poland. Nobody in Latin America hates Poland. They probably never met a Polish person. Even at their resorts, because Polish people don't go on vacation. They are poor. The only people that go on vacation are Western Europeans, Australians, Americans, and Japanese. Everybody else—if you see them in your country, they're not taking pictures. They're looking for restaurant work. Speaking of which, have you ever met a Wisconsinite at a resort? They don't go either. They'd stick out like a sore thumb. They aren't used to wearing shorts because it's too cold, and they don't sell bathing suits up there because you'd go out of business immediately. They wear shorts in forty-degree weather to show off their fat legs. They grill all the time.

Happy Days and *Laverne & Shirley* were both set in Wisconsin. The Fonz and the Cunninghams. The Big Ragu and Laverne DeFazio. The Big Ragu always bugged me. He was too clean-living for a tough guy. He never smoked or cursed or anything. He would burst into song, and that was fine, but the rest of it was too much. I prefer Lenny and Squiggy because they would come in and shout "Hello!" with this false sense of enthusiasm. They were really trying, even though their lives were wretched. You could tell just by looking at their cheap leather jackets and their slicked-back hair. And just the whine in their voices. They were sad, lonely men. Guys that got slapped around their whole lives by parents and other kids and then by their supervisors and the Big Ragus of the world and ultimately by the viewers as we all sat there and laughed at the false bravado and the vanquished hopes of these beaten dogs as they managed to gasp out one last cry to the gods for justice in that hello. And then it was back to being the awkward, perspiring outcasts.

Laverne & Shirley also said a lot about the angst of the late 1950s: the alienation of the blue-collar factory worker and the death of the American dream, if you really want to go there. The fact that they worked in the brewery made it Wisconsin, although the characters all had New York accents, which if I grew up in Wisconsin, I'm sure I'd be annoyed at. Today it would be mocked, but back then people were so impressed by TV and the rest of the country was so awed by Hollywood that you just bowed and appreciated the fact that it even acknowledged you. It was probably the beginning of the great schism between the coastal elite and the flyover states. And even today, they allowed some goofy Fonzie statue, almost as a further subjugation, to be bronze—like when Rome would put up a statue of Augustus Caesar and force the people of Brittany to walk by it all day. Or in Ireland, how the British flag makes them so angry. Even we plastic Paddies don't fly the Union Jack, unless you count my Who T-shirt in '76, but that's different. If you can't make an exception for the Who, then "who are you?" Ahahahahaha.

I always had a soft spot for Wisconsin because I was a Green Bay Packers fan when I was a kid.

The Packers are owned by the town like a co-op or something. It's the only socialist team. They'll probably have a picture of Bernie Sanders on their helmets next year. And they embrace the players too: when they score a touchdown, they have to jump into the stands and be engulfed by twelve German-American fatties and it's like having a twelve-armed German-goddess super nanny hugging you and telling you, "You haff done gut, *mein liebchen*!!" And that makes you feel like you can go out and conquer the world (poor choice of words when referring to Germans). Wisconsin is the state that you can rely on. The chubby friend who's good with electrical and, even if he doesn't know how to do something, goes on YouTube the night before and figures it out. And every country needs this.

★ ★ ★

MINNESOTA

LOOK BUSY

When I think of you, I think of a tall, high-cheekboned blonde. Like Alexander Skarsgård. Or Charlize Theron. Just beautiful. Cold. Unemotional. Which is the same as cold. I don't know why I just said it twice—maybe because they're cold. I think of Minnesotans that way even though I've been there a few times and there didn't seem to be a lot of tall, beautiful, cold, unemotional people there. A lot of average-looking people in Minnesota. Not fat like Wisconsin, but not thin like Norway. Although I've never been to Norway. But let's get back to Minnesota. What can you say about people whose idea of a vacation is renting a shack on a frozen lake and carving out glory holes for fish?

The first time I went to Minnesota, I was doing comedy in the 90s. And I went to the Mall of America and that's when I knew the country was on its way out. By the fact that the Mall of America was apparently something to be proud of instead of ashamed of. Malls were the downfall of this country in my opinion. Not minimalls, believe it or not. Indoor malls. Where you walk in and suddenly you are no longer part of the town. People being part of a town is important. You can see what everybody's up to. I know it's intrusive. That's why malls became popular: the idea of small-town living and everybody being up in your business was annoying people. The small town became the villain in the 60s. It started with *Peyton Place* because part of the 60s was a revolution against conformity. Then every movie and TV show was set in a small town trying to stop people or destroy people for being individual. I guess it peaked in 1984 with *Footloose,* where the religious people wanted to stop dancing because a kid died in a car crash after a dance. And then it just became an accepted trope that small towns were small-minded, and in every movie the person had to get out of the small town and they leave and the people behind are scrunching their faces at the end as the star laughs on a bus out of there. Those were simpler times, when the hero would leave on a bus and that would be considered a victory. Now if you leave on a bus, everybody thinks you're a loser.

But back when malls replaced small towns in the 70s, "impersonal" was a positive thing. Suburban sprawl was considered good. The mall killed personal interaction. And then the internet took it to the next level, of course. The Mall of America—the biggest mall in the world—being in Minnesota was no accident. Because Minnesota is an impersonal place. They don't ask you about your business; they don't want to get to know you better. They are the essence of Scandinavian culture. They want to work and then go home and do DIY projects around the house. Preferably wood-based. They were the last state to say "I love you" to their kids. It's not that Minnesotans don't love their kids; they just believe you say it through work. Actions speak louder than words. I had a friend, Mike Spillane, who married a Minnesota girl, and he said at the Sunday get-togethers the women would be in the kitchen and the guys would go in the other room, but they couldn't just sit and talk or watch the game because that wasn't acceptable. They would have to have something to fix. The host of the house would have to bring out something that needed to be repaired and they would all gather around it. That's pretty amazing. That's when you understand how the pioneers did it. They were people that actually looked down on leisure time. People who didn't want to spend their whole lives talking. The pioneers and Minnesotans looked at talking without working as a sin.

★ ★ ★

KANSAS

AUNT KANSAS

Kansas had a hell of a time becoming who they are. It was all during the 1850s and Missouri was attacking them and stuffing the ballot box to make Kansas a slave state. But Kansas brought out John Brown, the abolitionist hit man, and he killed a few Missourians, which brought everybody to their senses. That's what Kansas wants, ultimately: everybody brought to their senses. Saying someone was sensible was considered a hot compliment back in the day. It was like saying someone has a six-pack today. Kansas is one of those states that lives by farming law. All the Midwest is about farm law. Plant, harvest, early to bed, read the good book. That's what nobody seems to realize now. You don't look at the system or the law the same way other people might—it depends on your daily experience and routine. And if you get up at 5 A.M. and work on a tractor, you are going to have a different viewpoint than if you get up at 7 and get on the train to go to the metropolis and sit at a desk. Neither one is superior, just different.

Kansas always has a great basketball team. I don't know why some states love basketball and other states love football. Kansas is not known for schoolyards and sidewalks—it's known for plains and fields. So it's not the urban thing. But they love hoops and don't care about football. Just like Kentucky, Indiana, and North Carolina. Someone should do a study on why those states love B-ball more than football. Maybe I can do a *30 for 30* about it. Probably won't happen. But well worth a ponder. And that's what you can do in Kansas. You can ponder. Not talk. But ponder. Quietly, to yourself, while you are replacing the bags on your thresher.

Kansas is the center of the United States. And they have *The Wizard of Oz*. If they were smart, they'd make Kansas the gay-tourist destination that it could be. Set up a Disneyland-like yellow brick road and then have the houses and Munchkinland and the witch's castle. It would be a hot spot. Or they might do it and make it cheeseball. But either way, *The Wizard of Oz* is a look at how people used to look at Kansas. Tornados, which it still has. Wheat fields, which it still has. And that sentimental family-and-friends thing, which no place has. Auntie Em!

Kansas represents the strict, orderly, unmarried aunt who keeps everybody in line! The old spinster, but she's got a good heart underneath—she just gets a little cranky because she's never had sex. She's not a lot of fun, but when you need a warm bed and a hot meal, you go to her house. And it's always orderly. And if you need a couple of bucks, she'll make you do a couple of chores for it because she doesn't like handouts, but she'll give it to you. So that's pretty much Kansas. They have the same rules that spinster aunt has. No sex under their roof. No cursing. No leisure activities. You have to go to church, even though she knows you don't take it seriously. And you have to get a part-time job. Idle hands are the devil's workshop. Kansas is about productivity. If you want to talk and gossip, that's a luxury that is for the old retired people outside the general store or at the local greasy spoon. Kansas is all about humility even at the height of 70s rock 'n' roll. When other bands were singing about partying and debauching, the chorus of Kansas's rock hit was "All we are is dust in the wind."

★ ★ ★

NEBRASKA

ALONE IN A CROWDED ROOM

There's a lot of time for contemplation in Nebraska. Every time I go out there, it's the same thing: *What are we going to do?* And I've only been there for three hours!! I'm visiting. You run out of things to do in three hours in Nebraska. Don't ask me why. I don't know. It's just, you start staring at the damn horizon and start to get a little dazed.

Two electrical linemen in western Nebraska discovered the Columbian Mammoth in 1962, which was the world's largest woolly mammoth at the time. Pretty scary—something 22,000 pounds running around. But maybe not that scary, because I feel like the big beasts didn't really go after humans since they were all vegans. If you were standing next to a plant, they would stomp you, I guess, just to get at it.

Nebraska isn't vegan. They have those runza sandwich places, where they sell some kind of ground Germanic beef, cabbage, and onions on a roll—it's pretty tasty. I give them credit: they keep it to themselves like true Nebraskans do. They don't try to inflict it on the rest of the country like Philly cheesesteaks or po'boys from Louisiana. Because most places, all they do is try to get you to like their food. You go to St. Louis and they start barking about their barbecue before you get off the goddamn plane. You go to New Orleans, everything you eat they take credit for. Even in Massachusetts, they harass you to try the lobster roll. Hey, stop taking credit for it—you wouldn't even have it without Maine! You don't have lobster; you just added the bread and butter!! Shut your face.

Nebraska plays it close to the vest. They have the runza sandwich, and if you want one you come to Nebraska. They're not going to let some slick Michael Keaton type like in *The Founder* come and wreck the whole vibe just to squeeze a few trillion bucks out of it.

Nebraska loves football. They have no pro teams because it's too frivolous, but they do have the one college team that the whole state goes to watch at that big stadium. I mean, a lot of places feel that way about football, but it's significant in Nebraska because they don't do anything else as a leisure activity. The gym for the football team is known to have the largest weight room in the world. But you go to any one of those half-empty states and they have gyms and health clubs that are half a mile long. There's fifty feet between treadmills and you have to MapQuest if you want to find the spin class. Meanwhile in New York, people are stretching on top of each other on the mats, and yoga classes are held in the steam rooms. And that's not the only thing held in the steam rooms—but that's part of why they can charge $200 a month in membership fees.

Nebraska also has more miles of river than any other state, but it doesn't matter because it's not famous for that. If you're not known for something, no one is going to come see it, even if it's the best. You have to get a reputation as the River State. Maybe change your license plate. A license plate is the best publicity you can have and it's free. Once people say, "Ohhhhh, the River State," then you hit them with a couple of stupid commercials of blond people frolicking in the pristine waters of the Nebraska rivers. I know people think it's racist to say blond people, but guess what? People like to see blond people in a tourism commercial. It makes you feel like, "Well, if blond people go there, it must be pretty nice because they have their choice of locations—they can go pretty much anywhere." So screw me for being a cynical, hardened advertising expert. If Jon Hamm said it, you'd all be calling him a genius. The point is bigger than rivers. The point is, once your state is known for it, that's it. Look at Colorado. They are known to smoke weed. Even though it's legalized everywhere, Colorado was the first and now that's their reputation. Everybody wants some Colorado weed. Same with rivers. To visit a river, you go to Idaho or Montana. Meanwhile Nebraska says, "We are the river capital of the world." But nobody cares, including Nebraska. They want to be left alone. That should be their license plate: "We want to be alone."

They invented Kool-Aid in Nebraska. Everybody uses that expression, "drinks the Kool-Aid," which is derogatory, like you are brainwashed, all because Jim Jones got his followers to kill themselves by drinking Kool-Aid. I'm sure Kool-Aid hated that day and loved it too. There must have been some corporate meeting the day after the Jonestown mass suicide, one of those brainstorming sessions.

ROGER

We just found out a cult leader killed a congressional delegation and then also made his followers kill themselves with poisoned Kool-Aid. Ideas? John?

JOHN

Well, we could have the guy on the Kool-Aid packet not smile on the next shipment? Maybe he's got a tear streaming down in a different flavor?

ROGER

Bill?

BILL

We could add a black-licorice flavor to show we are in mourning?

ROGER

Don?

DON

What about we put together a picture of how wishy-washy Hawaiian Punch and Yoo-hoo drinkers are and then show the Jamestown soft focus—you understand, bodies—and talk about brand loyalty to the end? How our people ride and die with Kool-Aid?

ROGER

That's not an expression here in 1978, Don.

If you want to understand who Nebraska is, just look at Johnny Carson. Johnny Carson is probably the most famous Nebraskan: he had a real Nebraska personality underneath the Hollywood glitz. Yes, he was charismatic and funny and a party animal and a playboy, but underneath he was giving that Nebraskan lonely, faraway gaze the whole time. He could be sitting there with Burt Reynolds and Angie Dickinson and the band and the audience and millions at home laughing it up and we all loved him and it seemed like he loved all of us back, but you looked into his eyes and he was all by himself. And that's Nebraska.

★ ★ ★

NORTH DAKOTA

THE STATE NOBODY KNOWS

You fracking bastards, you had two good years with the oil boom, but you end up being *The Beverly Hillbillies*. That was a show where these in-breds struck oil and moved out to California and bought a mansion and basically ran roughshod over Beverly Hills. It was the wishful-thinking version of *The Grapes of Wrath*. A comic version of Steinbeck written by all the guys who couldn't get staff jobs on *Bewitched*. And the guys that couldn't get jobs on *Bewitched* had to do punch-up for *Hogan's Heroes* and *F Troop*: shit rolls downhill in every business. It was the golden age of the gallows-humor sitcom. Concentration camps, starving Dust Bowl migrants, and the Native American genocide were the ideal setups for family humor on TV back then. That was coming off the 50s sitcoms like *The Honeymooners,* where an embittered, rageful bus driver ended every episode by threatening domestic violence against his wife while the studio audience nudged each other in recognition. "That's just like you, honey, when you get mad," the wife would say and then limp back out to the 2 train, back up to the unheated three and half rooms they shared with four kids and an alcoholic uncle until they could save enough to buy a tract house in Suffolk County, and then spend the rest of their lives bitterly laughing at the people that got stuck on the wrong side of Jerome Avenue once the 60s hit. But I digress. Fracking made you big, North Dakota. They say you can't get blood from a stone, but you got oil from a rock, which is even harder.

Listen, I have nothing against you. And I have nothing for you either. I have no feelings about you. And I don't like that because we are both a part of this country. But I feel like you aren't even trying sometimes. You are just up there and—I don't know—at least South Dakota has Mount Rushmore. Why don't you do something like that? Do you even have mountains? See, I don't even know. There are so few pictures of you. You're a blank slate. And some people might think, well, that's a good thing. I've never even been to you. I don't think I will ever get there. I might die before I visit you. Who wants to die in North Dakota? Maybe General Custer or Sitting Bull? Even *they* died in South Dakota. So I know you have a long and illustrious history. Legend has it you were admitted into the union as a favor to Canada because they were getting nervous that you might want to become part of their country.

I looked at some pictures on Trip Advisor of your state capital, Bismarck. You gotta be shitting me. In New York we call that Elmira, no offense to you or Elmira. There's not even a city hall! The mayor probably holds his meetings at the endless garden bar at Ruby Tuesday. Bismarck is a good place for the witness-protection program. There's probably been like five mob guys that killed themselves from living there after one too many trips to the Museum of Horseshoes or whatever halfhearted attempt at tourism you've come up with. They think the mob is the only worry they have until they get into Bismarck and try eating the Bismarck Applebee's three-cheese chicken penne when you grew up two blocks from Chazz Palminteri. The aftertaste will make them kill themselves faster than any hit man ever could.

You're not Cowboys and you're not Indians (sic). You're not Canada and you're not the United States. You are you. You could probably do some reality show there. North Dakotans struck it rich and then watched everybody spend it on belt buckles and show horses or whatever they did. I know they didn't save it. Nobody does when they get money. When I was on *Saturday Night Live,* I shouldn't have been throwing cash around like the black sheep in the Saudi royal family on a weekend in Belgium. Where he gets drunk and tries to buy up all the waffles just to prove a point to his strict father. But it happens. North Dakota never had money before. You know how many rappers ended up broke from the 80s? Guys that were so rich they couldn't walk in their own projects to visit family without it being a scene from *The Hurt Locker.* Your road manager is speaking into a walkie-talkie: "Old friend that helped you write lyrics for your first talent show and you never hooked him up at ten o'clock and his younger brother in the fifth-story breezeway about to throw spark plugs. Be advised."

But there is one contribution you made to this country, North Dakota: you made a man out of Teddy Roosevelt. I'll give you that. He was a sickly Ivy League nerd who was depressed after his mother died and so he went into "therapy," which in those days meant going out in the plains and shooting things. So you must be doing something right. Teddy always gave you a shout-out as a reason he became president. Also, you were Lewis and Clark's favorite state and they were state experts, so I guess I have to back off. Because Lewis and Clark were the original Yelp for states.

★ ★ ★

SOUTH DAKOTA

PLAYING DEADWOOD

Can you really look me in the eye and say you've given it your all to be a fun and interesting state? You are riding off the fact that North Dakota looks at you like you are the hip brother, but the rest of us have seen things and we know a dud when we meet one. Maybe being associated with North Dakota is holding you back? How about this? You change your name. Rebrand. West Minnesota. Anything. You're too plain Jane. You are annoying to a guy like me because peace and quiet are not my thing. I prefer a little excitement once in a while. I know what you're going to say: "Hey, you do you and I'll do me." Fair enough. But being a state should involve a little effort on your part. Look at other states and see what they do and then do that. I'm not saying imitate them, but get inspiration from them. Look at Nevada. They are a bunch of shitty dirt-filled plains like you and they brought in gambling and made themselves a destination. What about you? You probably thought Mount Rushmore would be the thing, but nobody's flocking to it. It was a good idea—I don't doubt it. But you only made four presidents. You should've made it every president's head. And each new one would have to come there during his term and model his head for the great sculpting. You may not like that idea, but at least I'm trying to think of something to help you out. And I don't even live there! But I'm trying. What are you doing?

You don't even have famous people from South Dakota. Tom Brokaw and Crazy Horse. Crazy Horse was probably the last exciting person who showed up in that state and he died in 1877. Just with what I've written in this one page I've given more thought to South Dakota than anyone in history. Maybe they like it like that. Some people don't like to be noticed. They don't want to stick out. Maybe there's a reason.

You do have Sturgis. You have the biker rally every year. Every August all the bikers in the country turn the Super 8 Motel into the opening scene from *The Warriors*. It's the only place where you can get your face kicked in while you're watching a girl in assless chaps dance unironically to Def Leppard. It's for the other one-percenters, not the ones who live on Park Avenue. Everybody in South Dakota had a neck tattoo before it was trendy. If you ask for a paper plate for your hot dog, they think you're gay. If you don't have fifteen fresh stitches in your face after the second day, they think you're a narc. It's one of those conventions where nobody has a name tag on their shirt but the patch on the back of their jacket tells you everything you need to know. Then the bikers spend the rest of the year talking about what happened those three days, I guess. They should make the Sturgis rally all year round, like a Vegas just for bikers. Then they should start carving all the rocks into faces and South Dakota will be a combination of Vegas and a tourist site for rock sculptors. Plus, rock climbers can climb on all the celebrity faces. You could have little kids learn rock climbing and history at the same time. A rock climb through American history. I know this is a great idea. And I will give it to you, South Dakota, because you've suffered enough in my humble opinion. So, here's what you do. You start training schools for rock carving and sculpting, or whatever it's called. Then you all stand under the mountain and you scream until there's an avalanche and it puts you out of your misery and we don't have to worry about being a bad parent anymore, because you don't exist. I'm just kidding. I'm from New York, so we're a little arrogant. But we had some bad years too. We went bankrupt in 1975. So I know the power dynamic can shift in a minute. You never know what's next. Look at North Dakota. For years they were the farmers who had no grass or water and then they hit it big with fracking. So don't give up! Your day may come!

★ ★ ★

THE
SOUTHWEST

Ya'll can go to hell, I'm going to Texas.
—Davy Crockett, after serving three terms
as a Tennessee congressman

America's addiction to expansion and fresh starts and promise and potential led us farther west. A lot of PTSD Civil War vets combined with
immigrants who worked the railroads started it. The railroad hired all
the workers, they made all the towns popular, and they brought all the
goods and trade back and forth. The railroads did to the stagecoach what
Uber did to taxis. So all sorts of people moved out there and there were
no houses! As a result, you had to create a society that was constantly
in motion. And that constant movement into unknown conditions also
created the personality that became known as American.

The urge to constantly move is why America invented the mobile
home. Almost as soon as cars came out, people said: I love this so much,
I never want to leave it. I want to eat in it and sleep in it and have sex in

it. All the big shots—Henry Ford, Edison, Firestone—went car camping in 1913. Because you wanted to be with nature but still connected to technology. And because we wanted to be individuals, we wanted that experience customized. In the Declaration of Independence there's a line about the right to alter government and if you can alter *government* if you are dissatisfied, of course you can alter a car. Or a motorcycle. Anything on wheels, really. Because we were the first society encouraged to stand out. Other society's people tried to blend in. Americans were allowed to show our creative side. In other civilizations, you had artists whose work you were allowed to view once everybody in the royal family got bored by their work. But in the United States we were all allowed to be our own artists. And the perfect place to be artists was on cars and motorcycles. We associated standing still with lack of progress. So we like our art in motion. The next time you see a motorcycle that's customized to look like Predator and the driver has a T-shirt that says INVEST IN PRECIOUS METALS—BUY LEAD with a picture of a bullet on it, he's not crazy. He's an artist.

There's a reason we have a subculture of survivalists. It's how we started. It's only one short step from camping to survivalists. The idea of living off the land is primal. And it was our recent past. We lived off the land, and then enough people living off the land lived off the same general patch of land so we ended up with a community. And whenever there's a group of people together, there are also a few thieves. So you need a system of justice. A posse, a courthouse, a jail. And when it got too big, the federal government would say, "You are no longer a territory— you are a state. When you have a problem, we will solve it. Whether it's troublemakers or pestilence or access to goods, we can help you. We will make sure the railroad stops near you." Because if you were near the railroad, you were going to get first dibs on everything. Most people liked that idea. Except the survivalists. The survivalists saw more people coming, and they don't like crowds. So they started moving farther west. We called survivalists "mountain men" in those days. "Hermits" in

Europe. Mountain men were like the early artists in Williamsburg who hated when all the hipsters moved in so they moved to Upstate in like 2007. And most people have a little survivalist in them in the United States. That's why camping is so popular. It's a dress rehearsal for the apocalypse.

It's natural that religious speakers would become popular in a place that's all about free speech. Even today. Even if some of them are hypocrites and frauds, their message is good. Let's be honest, they're entertaining too. If it's bread and circuses. They're kind of both, right? Aimee Semple McPherson, Jimmy Swaggart, John Wesley, Billy Sunday, Elmer Gantry.

It's been the same with our system of government since the moment Thomas Jefferson wrote "all men are created equal." Even if we haven't lived up to it, you can't disagree with the sentiment. And America is the place where from the 1800s to 1941 preachers were the only entertainment. There were dance hall shows, but that meant you had to go into a saloon, which meant people were going to hustle you. It was temptation. It was too shady unless you were a perverted prospector or a cattle rustler. Instead, you could see a faith healer—they had snakes and people that had limps five minutes ago that were now dancing around the aisles, everybody singing and moaning and speaking in tongues! You walk out smiling and sweating and you had to give a few coins, but it was cheaper than a saloon. It was church for people who had a wild side to them. They were too sexual for the United Methodist Church and too respectable for whorehouses and bars. Those were the only leisure activities if you were poor. Throughout history, the rich had foxhunting and musicians, but the poor had nothing except hangings and the church. The preachers were the only ones to talk to the poor. And then in America after World War II, we got to the point where even the poor could go to concerts and have leisure time. And the people in the South and West liked different leisure activities. They didn't like concerts. They liked rodeo and then it became motocross and funny cars and bike weeks—leisure, like anything else in this country, is about identity and choice. And sports. America made sports available to the masses. In the old days, it was croquet and court tennis, and sports were a sign of rich, decadent laziness. In the twentieth century, we made it okay not to work. For everybody. And there's no stigma attached to laziness. We smile and cheer when somebody is playing a sport. Or having fun. In the old days, nobody cheered at fun. Fun wasn't part of the equation. Even little kids had to work. Kids didn't have games. The only game a kid would play until 1908 was tag, to see who had to work the night shift at the mine that winter. People didn't have traditional vacations. A vacation was Sunday. And that's another reason preachers were so popular. Because instead of thinking about how miserable Monday was going to be, you could hear someone talk about how beautiful heaven was going to be.

To settle the West, you wanted people who were determined and a little bit insane. Damaged people with nothing to lose. You see those old John Wayne movies? They are all in a stagecoach. The prostitute, the drunken doctor, the orphan, the runaway slave, the rebellious teen—all brought together by John Wayne, who used to be in the army but committed some kind of atrocity during the Mexican-American War.

Settlers were many different types. You had the outdoors types. You had adventurers, who were probably ADD; you had religious types; you had weirdos; you had people running from the law, society, their families, themselves. You had people who just made everyone else uncomfortable. Probably about 20 percent of the people who went out West were severely damaged, dangerous, and perverted maniacs. If you were in the other 80 percent, you had to deal with these people. And you had to make sure they understood the consequences of harassing you. There were no cops or sheriffs. Just you and your weapons. So that created a personality. What they call frontier law. Where your gun is the cop, the lawyer, the jury, and the penitentiary. It all gets settled at high noon in a cloud of smoke. That's why they were called settlers. They would settle shit themselves. They'd say, "Sheriff, I'm having a problem with the ranch next to me. This guy is building his fence on my property." And the sheriff knew what you really were saying, which was, "Somebody is going to die in the next few days." The sheriff wouldn't try to resolve the dispute peacefully. His job was just to book Main Street at high noon for you on the next available date.

Gold rush, silver rush, land rush. A lot of rushing going on. Because when you heard the word "rush," you knew it was now or never. No hesitation. No time to think. You just packed up your wagon and moved out. And there was no going back once you left. Everybody knew that once you crossed the rivers and the mountains and used up all that money and that energy, you had to get rich or die trying, as they say. Maybe not rich as we define it today, but to "acquire" a plot of land. Get a house and a piece of property. And the farther west you went, the more you were saying, "I'm young and hip." Being in New York or Philadelphia was for immigrants. Being in Ohio and Kansas was for your parents. Being in Colorado or Arizona was hipster. It's just like New York: living in Williamsburg used to be hip, but now it's like living with your parents. Bushwick is like Indiana in 1840. And the Bronx is Colorado.

Everybody makes movies, but movies started here, and we're famous for action movies, which only started in the 1960s. Before that, we were famous for Westerns. The whole world loved Westerns. There was something very important about the town being bullied by the local gang and then hiring the loner who swore never to fight again but ended up blowing all the bad guys' brains out and then moving on. And those movies were also always about things that people came to associate with Americans. Your own land, a system of law, and guns. Those movies all said that our system of law didn't work, that you needed to bring in some shooters once in a while. They said that guns were the great equalizers, but you had to have the balls to pull the trigger. Not the most civilized message—but that was sort of the story of the West. And there was something about a stranger, and the stranger had to be a certain type. Tall: no short guys were allowed. Thin: nobody wanted a fatty to save their town. Only the local banker was allowed to be a fatty. And the stranger was quiet: no big talkers. In those movies the big talker was the cattle baron, who was behind all this shit. He was from back east!! He was out there talking people out of their land. Land was what everybody wanted. Even the stranger, except he wanted land out past where civilization was. If they were in Kansas, he was trying to get to Montana; if they were in Montana, he was trying to get to Nevada; if they were in Nevada, he was trying to get to Arizona. The stranger was a survivalist.

Trump has that cattle-baron personality. A maniac, a braggart, and a chaotic troublemaker, but when you ask half this country whether they would rather have that or the town banker, they would say the cattle baron. Because the banker is a slick talker and a sneak. And some people feel the cattle baron and the banker are in league with each other. But there are no other choices even in Westerns. Ultimately, the gunfighter is just working for one or the other. Billy the Kid, Wyatt Earp, Bat Masterson—they were hired guns. Emphasis on the word "hired." So even those guys were on the take, were part of the system.

TEXAS

THE NEW YORK OF THE SOUTH

What is it about Texas? I can give you my opinion, but Texas doesn't care. They stopped caring what the "North" said a long time ago. Look at Six Flags over Texas: they're including on equal footing, the U.S. Flag with France, Spain, etc. It's a very marginalizing thing. They are the capital of the South. But they are also the capital of the Southwest somehow. I've talked to people from New Mexico, and I go, "What do you think about climate change?" and they go, "I don't know—talk to Texas." Same with Mississippi: you ask them a question, they tell you "talk to Texas." And Texas was the last state in the South. And they still ended up in charge, because they actually were their own country.

Texas is the daddy of the South. And daddies are a big thing down there. Mommies are big in the Northeast, but it's daddies down south. Dads take their sons hunting and teach them to throw a football. Up North, you only see your father every other weekend and then he takes you to his depressing apartment and you order in Chinese food and he doesn't have real plates or utensils. And no ice cubes, so the soda is warm. The tray is just out there on top of the dishwasher. But Texans bond with their sons. They take them hunting and give them initials for a name. "Now see here, J. C., you got to make sure to adjust the scope or the sight ain't in line when you trying to kill an armadillo." They have to hunt weird shit down there because there's no forest, so you have to make do with desert animals. But the truth is, all that the Texas daddies really want is to have a son who can be a good high school quarterback. Even a lineman is fine. If their kid is chubby, all the other fathers comment at the barbecue, "I tell you what. He gonna make one hell of a left tackle."

High school football is the only thing that matters in Texas. Even college or the pros means nothing compared with high school. Because you can still the approach the kid—he still eats in the cafeteria and puts his pads on one leg at a time—but by the time they get to college, these quarterbacks are bigger divas than I am. You try to take them to an Outback Steakhouse, they look at you like, "Outback? I don't eat at Outback." "Oh, excuse me, Colt. Two years ago you thought Red Robin was a Gordon Ramsay restaurant, you little fuck."

Football is the key to Texas. Even in Austin they have tailgate parties in the back of their Kia plug-in hybrids. They do shots of fermented tea and grill lemon-pesto vegetable skewers. While next to them some hick family in from Fredericksburg has a squirrel impaled on a spit in the back of the F-150. But they both love football!

A tailgate party is a way of doing a lot of things: showing off your new truck, showing off your hot MILF, and bonding with other people in similar vehicles with similar MILFs. The difference between tailgate parties in New Jersey, where I've been to them, and everywhere else is that people don't curse at tailgate parties anywhere else. In the parking lot at MetLife, a lot of people are screaming before the game. It's disconcerting and makes me want to rip the antennas off their cars and slice their faces with them. But a tailgate party in a place like Texas is half Super Bowl party, half church picnic. A lot of tucked-in shirts and boots and everybody's wearing stonewashed jeans and jewelry. That's another thing about Texas. They like their bling. Even if they are broke, they put on the show: 30,000-dollar millionaires, they call them. They understand that nobody likes to be around poor people. "If you don't have it, fake it!!" That's the state motto.

But there's nothing mediocre about the GST. Great State of Texas. Oh, they do things in a big way. First, with their cattle ranches, where they rode around on horses all day, branding dumb beasts with hot irons. Every movie from 1945 to 1960 was about a cattle rancher vs. a bunch of desperadoes. Which is fine, but annoying when all the great filmmakers like Scorsese act like those are the best movies of all time. Listen, Marty, you loved it because you were twelve years old, just like I love Tommy James and the Shondells because it brings back that time in my life. That doesn't mean *The Man from Laramie* is *The 400 Blows*, you longing-for-the-more-innocent-time-of-your-childhood sad sack. But the plains of Texas were a real thing, and course they had the conflict between the old character and the young idealist cowboy in every John Wayne movie:

JOHN WAYNE
Well, partner, looks like there's some redskins out there.

YOUNG COWBOY
The toxic masculinity is thicker than the methane from the cattle, and if I hear one more dismissive remark about the people whose land we're taking, I am going to scream.

JOHN WAYNE
Well, I didn't know you were a savage-lover. Maybe you should put on some war paint and go join 'em.

YOUNG COWBOY
Wait, seriously? That's your answer? Put on war paint because I tell you

that maybe you're acting like a maniac driving cattle through
people's lands and shooting them when they show up
and complain? This is going to be a great drive.

And then the oil boom. Which ended—I'm still not sure why? People are still using oil in their cars, no thanks to Elon Musk. It was on for the whole twentieth century for H. L. Hunt, Clint Murchison, and all those loud-talking, rich, backslapping, hard-drinking, ten-gallon-hat guys. Then they got "too big for their britches" and they sent their kids like George W. to Yale, where they lost their identity and their street cred. Suddenly guys are cleaning deer in cable-knit sweaters and, just like that, they went from gunfights at the O.K. Corral to heated dorm debates with the Winklevoss twins.

Somehow, they all managed to unite to kill JFK. Well, they didn't kill him. But if I get punched in your bar, you are still liable. And by the way those police reacted when Jack Ruby shot the guy in front of them was right out of a silent film, mugging like the snooty hotel manager in a Charlie Chaplin movie. But I don't think Lyndon Johnson—who was a real Texan—actually planned it. I think his assistant probably started to tell him that he'd been hearing rumors but then LBJ cut him off midsentence and grabbed him by the shoulders and said, "I wear the boots so when I step in the horseshit, I don't feel it," or some aphorism that feels Texas-ish. But anyway, the Kennedy assassination was probably the worst moment in American history and we will never know what really happened, but the deed is done and the die is cast. And Dallas had a black mark on its soul for eight years until Tom Landry led a band of Christians and cokeheads to the national championship and they became America's team.

But Texas oil has affected the state, because as I said there's no greenery. It's all cement. You think I'm lying? Go to Houston or Dallas or San Antonio and try to Instagram a picture of yourself standing next to a tree. You can't do it. Even in Austin—the hippie kid in the family—they don't even have trees! But Austin is what I call an outlier (an annoying word of the early twenty-first century), because it's right in the heart of Texas but they like to rebel against the rest of Texas. They are Steve Earle Texas. They hate Texas but they hate the North too. They can insult Texas, but if anyone else does they go, "Well now, pardner, I don't 'preciate that." They go right into "pardner mode" like they just shot their way out of the Alamo.

Texas is always threatening independence, which gives you a lot of leverage. It could backfire too—look what happened to Diane from *Cheers;* I mean I know it was a long time ago, but still. My point is that Texas has a lot of well-trained soldiers, so if they did decide to leave, they might take all that expensive military gear with them and that's gonna cost us. And they will probably take Oklahoma with them, because they need somebody to abuse. So to Texas I say, *Vaya con Díos* if you leave, but we need you to stay to keep up appearances, at least for the near future. We have to present a united front at the UN or people will start saying, "America's falling apart." I understand you and California want to get your own apartments, but at least wait till the house is paid off. I understand Texas, because I'm from New York. Texas has the same attitude as New York. They think they're doing everybody else a favor by being part of America. Sorry, other 48; it's just how we are.

ARIZONA

THE INSTAGRAM-MODEL

Arizona became the 48th state in 1912. They took their time, huh? Hey, Arizona, are you sure? We don't want to put you out. Arizona is a model state. By "model" I mean it's beautiful but empty. It doesn't have highways—it has runways. It is one of those places that is just blessed with good looks, but it hasn't really done anything with them. You know, what are they supposed to do, have a state fair? Leave that for the fatties up in Iowa and Indiana. People don't want to build anything in Arizona because it's already beautiful. It's like other states have to work to attract people, but Arizona just has to stand there and people wanna buy them drinks. The tourist board in New Jersey or Oklahoma has to take pictures at the right angle and use the right Instagram filters because they know they need to hide some of their flaws. Arizona was hot even before people heard about the Grand Canyon.

It's funny, though, because even though Arizona's supposed to be arm candy for the country, they have somehow involved themselves with politics in a big way. They're very rambunctious. There's always some drama down there, and it starts with the way the West was won. It's that Billy the Kid/Tombstone gunfighter personality that Arizona still has in their genes.

A lot of the state is caved in. Salt mines, canyons, craters—the state is just always trying to trip you up. I've spent time in the cities in Arizona, but never been to the damn Grand Canyon. I feel like it's one of those things that you need to see, but you also have to go down into it on a donkey or something. I'm not just going to go and take a picture and then look at it for a minute and go, "Wow," and leave, like Chevy Chase in *Vacation*. But then again, I can see planning a trip and then getting there and suddenly I'm on top of a donkey in 100-degree heat sweating in my sombrero going, *This was a mistake.* In the 1870s it was different. Once you got to Arizona, you weren't coming back. You were committed for life. It wasn't like going to the farming states or to California. You went to those states to be in a community or strike gold. There was no gold or cattle in Arizona. People went out there to live on a ranch and raise God knows what. Lizards? There are no animals unless you count coyotes and prairie dogs, which I don't.

They had copper mines, so I guess that was popular back in the days when pennies were big. They still make them, but just because it's a tradition, even though they're nothing now. When I was a little kid, pennies still meant something. Even when adults dropped a penny, they'd pick it up. Now a five-year-old kid drops a quarter, he's like, "Fuck it." So copper can't be the reason people went out there. It was the weather. And the gunfights. People went out there for gunfights and maybe just to relax. Gunfights were the only spectator sport back then. High noon, you'd be peeking behind the saloon doors or out the windows and the deputy would be standing there with some cocksucker who was trying to ruin the town, and I'm sure there was wagering. Then they'd bust out the guns and you'd either cheer or you'd go, "Uh-oh, the bad guy won." Now what would we do? Somebody would say, "We have to hire a gunfighter." And they'd send some kid on a horse to find a gunfighter. And the bad guy would be walking around with his gang for a few weeks terrorizing people and saying, "I know you people probably hired a gunfighter to come here and try to kill me" and they'd go, "No we did not. We love the way you are acting." Then the gunfighter would show up and there'd be another shootout and then the bad guy would be shot and you'd pay the gunfighter and he'd ride off into the sunset like Jon Taffer on *Bar Rescue*.

The weather *is* pretty sweet in Arizona. It's always sunny. But there's no ocean. No lakes. No rivers. Just the Petrified Forest, the Painted Desert. The Petrified Forest is between Apache country and Navajo country. There's still a lot of both of those tribes out there. When I was a kid, the Apaches were the ones in every movie and TV show. I'm sure the other tribes were a little annoyed that the Apaches were always considered the baddest of the bad. And the other tribes were either the sellouts or the victims. Apaches had a cool name, and that was it. They even had a couple of stars: Geronimo and Cochise. I'm sure the other tribes had some great potential warriors, but they didn't have the training program the Apaches had. Or maybe they didn't have the high ground, and the Apaches did. Arizona is the Wild West. The reason they got so many violent pricks out there is because it was on a route for the California gold rush and then silver became big and then a bunch of Texans that didn't do well in Texas came and started rustling cattle and taking over ranches. Every state had that element of good, hardworking people followed by thieves who got run out of some other state. It's kind of sad that we are supposed to be *United* States but that each state would go to their lowlifes, "Hey, why don't you go to Arizona; they'll probably love you there!" We like to pass our problems along. Eventually, a few generations in, Arizona has that David Spade personality. Kind of laid-back and sun-drenched and you can't really tell if they are being sarcastic or what. Arizona, the rattlesnake with the heart of silver.

OKLAHOMA

PTSD

Oklahoma is home to the most casinos in the United States, which is due to the rather uncomfortable fact of the Trail of Tears ending in Oklahoma. The Five Tribes—Cherokee, Choctaw, Seminole, Chickasaw, and Creek—were marched out of their ancestral lands and sent out to what was called Indian country, which is Oklahoma. A lot of people died on that journey. Andrew Jackson's Indian Removal Act started it off and then after Jackson, Martin Van Buren kept it up, but MVB was basically the spineless sidekick to Jackson. Jackson was the Michael Myers of presidents. You couldn't kill him. People shot him and the guns misfired, he would beat them with his hickory stick (Jackson's nickname, Old Hickory, came from the way he did that, just like a mob guy who hits people with a Louisville Slugger is nicknamed Bats), and he got shot once in the chest by a rival and just put his hand over his chest and shot the other guy dead. Jackson was a real lightning rod for assassination. All the senators hated him; he was like Julius Caesar only luckier (obviously). But he went ahead with the Indian Removal Act,

even though many people, including Davy "King of the Wild Frontier" Crockett, opposed it. Davy Crockett hated Jackson and said that if
Jackson's chosen successor, Martin Van Buren, got elected, he was going
to leave the country (sound familiar?). Only Crockett actually did. He
moved to Texas, which was at that point an independent nation, and
then got killed at the Alamo.

But the Trail of Tears ended in Oklahoma. The name Oklahoma
is Choctaw for "red people." But at least the tribes had their own land,
right? Not for long. To add insult to injury, the United States had a land
rush in 1889, and everybody that wanted to was allowed to move in.
And a lot of people decided to bum-rush Oklahoma before they even
announced it, and they were called Sooners because of that. Too Sooners
is what we would call them today.

Oklahoma also got the worst of it during the 1930s Dust Bowl.
Down south even the national disasters sound like a college football
championship game. Strong winds, drought, clouds of dust, and locusts
destroyed the ecology. If you ever read *The Grapes of Wrath,* you know the
story. They go out west to pick fruit and end up getting their asses kicked.
All the farmers had to move to California, so you ended up with a lot of
Central California hicks, like Merle Haggard.

Oklahoma is just dwarfed by Texas. Because Texas is loud and big.
And Oklahoma is their little brother. Oklahoma has oil too, but not as
much. They have a couple of good college football teams, sure, but Texas
has about eleven.

Their state flower is mistletoe, which is pretty perverted. You are getting a cheap feel on anybody who comes in the state with the best of
intentions when they go to see the state flower.

Oklahoma, the number one producer of alabaster. Drywall. They can
drywall the whole state. I know every state has to have its thing, but they
are grasping at straws with this one. Apologies to the sea turtles for that
expression. Oklahoma has alabaster caves there from 200 million years
ago. It is kind of cool, though. To think that it was around during the

end of the Paleozoic era—all those days of fire and ice and the planet when it was forming is pretty badass for some reason. I like to think about those days. Nobody was here yet. It was just a bunch of giant eggs and mammals with weird horns and birds with giant noses and turtles, which are odd looking enough today.

Then it all ended with the extinction: 96 percent of marine and 70 percent of terrestrial species died out. It took ecosystems 30 million years to come back. And what does this have to do with Oklahoma? Maybe their PTSD was one of those things that is built into the earth itself. If trauma can be genetic, maybe so can earthly trauma and upheaval. And maybe the Dust Bowl was a flashback that Oklahoma was having to the Permian-Triassic extinction. Because why else would it act like that? Like a temporary repressed memory that comes out of nowhere, like when something causes a person to overreact because it triggers something from their past. Oklahoma is our temporary repressed memory of the Trail of Tears and the Tulsa Massacre. It's ironic that they have the most casinos because historically they don't seem to be very lucky.

★ ★ ★

NEW MEXICO

BREAKING BORED

The federal government said to New Mexico in 1945, "We need a place to test atomic bombs and we'd like to try them out on you." And New Mexico said, "Um . . . Okay, I guess." That's the definition of low self-esteem. New Mexico has had problems from day 1. First, its name. New York or New Jersey or New England were all named after places that were an ocean away. So it's almost endearing that they got those names. It's an expression of homesickness. It's almost sweet (in a colonialist way). But to name a place after a place right next door is lazy and inconsiderate to both places. It's just, we don't care about you. And that's New Mexico's problem. Nobody cares about them. Nobody even mentioned them until *Breaking Bad* and *Better Call Saul*. Who wants to be known for a meth-dealing teacher and a corrupt lawyer? New Mexico, apparently. They would probably rather be known for their flora and fauna (still not sure what those words refer to), but instead they are known for great but bizarre TV shows. Oh well, you don't have a choice when you are New Mexico. They have zero natural resources, no water, no plant life, and even the cities are made of adobe. I think. They have Play-Doh houses. The kids probably try to eat them. Imagine you come home and your whole garage is eaten by your kids. You can't even get mad because if you tell anybody, they just think it's cute. But back to *Breaking Bad*. I drove through New Mexico once, and it was pretty beautiful. And then I got to Albuquerque and there was a drive-by shooting next to my hotel. I fell out of bed like I had just gotten shot myself. So I get it. New Mexico is a bipolar state.

New Mexico is also home to the Lincoln County land wars, which were infamous among the many territorial gunslinger battles. These were the only competitions before professional sports, so you would choose sides. And the biggest name was Billy the Kid. Because he was young it made it more appealing to people. Billy the Kid skipped college and went right into the pros. And then Pat Garrett was the man who hunted him down all over New Mexico for years and caught him and he escaped and then found out where he was staying and killed him in that house one night. And that made Billy the Kid more popular and everybody turned on Pat Garrett because of ageism. But the point is that they were the first great rivalry, like Larry Bird and Magic Johnson rekindled interest in the NBA. They brought a resurgence in the popularity of gunfighting battles.

They also have the most Ph.D.s of any state in the country. Per capita. But since there's only eighty people in the whole state, that's only four Ph.D.s, that's not as impressive. Okay, so let's say it's more than that. It still makes no sense. What are these Ph.D.s in? Probably nuclear something. Or maybe they're geological Ph.D.s in Carlsbad Caverns. I wouldn't mind going to those. That would be pretty cool to be in there. But not on a tourist trip, alone at night. How crazy would that be? You have to get in there with all those ghosts of the Apaches or ancient medicine women who appear in the frozen waterfall. And then the next morning, they find you dead with stalactites drilled through your chest and they think they fell off the cave and impaled you, but they never know. But meanwhile you start haunting people. No, most of the Ph.D.s are probably for nuclear stuff. That's New Mexico.

Mexico used to have all these states. Obviously, New Mexico is the most personal to them because of the taunting name. They lost the Southwest to the United States in the Treaty of Guadalupe Hidalgo, which is like all of those treaties after a war. The winner writes up a treaty and the loser has to sign it or else. Can you imagine losing a war and then the winners come and hand you a piece of paper and you look at it and laugh and rip it up? Well, back to New Mexico. I am still amazed they survived a self-inflicted nuclear attack. They are like those cutters. They are full of self-hate and they think they're ugly, so they nuked themselves. They did what the whole country is doing now, destroying ourselves from within.

THE WEST

Leave me alone or let me go to hell by my own route.
—CALAMITY JANE

This country was like any other married couple. When it was good, it was great. But when we had fights, it was usually about money.

Most Americans agree: Abraham Lincoln was our greatest president. Or the least hated president. But even he screwed up with the Homestead Act of 1862. He told everybody to go west and claim land if they wanted it. That's not something you say to a bunch of human beings with all the faults of greed, desire, delusion, etc. That's like throwing a bunch of money in the street and saying, "You'll work it out among yourselves." Yeah, after a lot of fighting and bloodshed. But that's how they thought in those days. They let nature take its course, I guess. It was like herd immunity. Lincoln was all preoccupied with the Civil War. He probably said, "Let these people go out there and claim the land and after the war they will have to be part of the union because I hooked them up." And he knew they'd face a lot of hostile Indian tribes, but they'd already seen that through every area of the United States, so by the time the West was the frontier it was a given, as horrible as that sounds. They knew the drill. They knew they were going to have a fort nearby that would come to help them if they heard about an attack. But they also knew they had to be prepared to fight and maybe die. Everybody probably knew it was fifty-fifty that you were going to get murdered or die in a natural disaster. Lincoln was lucky that people didn't have a tendency towards lawsuits in those days. Today, people would've canceled Lincoln for every misfortune that befell them personally because they followed the Homestead Act. Not to mention all the "range wars" that more or less gave the western people their personality. The wars are depressing for many reasons. Number one, how people can kill each other even over empty land. The place was almost deserted, yet the cattlemen and the homesteaders went to war. It was mostly greed on the part of the cattle ranchers, but the homesteaders also hooked up with cattle rustlers like Billy the Kid. And if you were hanging out with Billy the Kid, then even if you meant well, you were going to get involved in shady things. Just like the unions had to partner with the mafia to survive back in the 1930s.

A lot of territories only became states after bloodshed so there was a lot of ratification by Second Amendment.

Fence-Cutting Wars. In Texas. "Big Pasture" became a thing. Because the Homestead Act of 1862 said any farmer that would move out west would get 160 acres. Sounded great, but it's hard to keep control of people, not to mention measurements out there, so you had people killing each other over fence cutting. Because that's property lines. It may sound primitive, but if somebody steps in front of you in line at the store, don't you want to hurt them?

The Sheep Wars. (No sex jokes, please.) These led to the Deep Creek murders on the border of Idaho and Nevada. Overgrazing was the main worry. Basically, overeating would get you a bullet in the head. If you had a sheep who didn't know when to say when, it could cost you your life.

Railroad Wars took place in Colorado, Oklahoma, Kansas, and California. It started when the railroad would build through certain towns but not stop there. That's the ultimate insult when all everybody wanted was to be acknowledged and get mail. After railroads came around, nobody wanted a stagecoach stop.

County-Seat Wars. In Kansas, this was another rich guy who tried to force his town of Ingalls to be the county seat, and he hired thugs like Wyatt Earp and Bat Masterson (who I always thought were good guys, but I guess they were just what they said they were, hired guns) to intimidate and kill the voters. Bat and Wyatt were celebrities by that point too, so they probably had an attitude like, "We do what we want, to who we want, when we want." But the townspeople of Cimarron, where the county seat was, were apparently no softies; they stood there with guns and pitchforks and threatened to burn down the other town and kill all their citizens. Wow! But it shows how people reacted when you tried to influence their vote. And to think: now two-thirds of people in the United States won't vote because it's raining or they want to finish watching *The Masked Singer*. Meanwhile people in those days were willing to draw down on two of arguably pound-for-pound the best gunslingers in history so all the old ladies in your town can count votes.

Salt Wars. There was even a salt war in West Texas. People will fight over anything, but when there's money involved, it gets extra bloody. Everybody wants to say, "That's America." No. That's the planet. You could go anywhere in history and whenever anybody says, "Look what we found," everybody else wants some. And if they can't find their own source, they try to take yours. Or if they do find it, they try to keep it all.

Egg Wars. Took place outside San Francisco during the gold rush. Yes, people killed each other trying to control the egg market in San Francisco. That's why there's so many vegans in San Francisco now. Bad memories.

Coal Wars. Lots of those. They were mostly on the East Coast. Harlan County, Kentucky. Battle of Blair Mountain in West Virginia. Largest American armed uprising since the Civil War. The Molly Maguires in Pennsylvania. These guys would end up bombing the mines. Because as in any other group, there was peer pressure. There were guys that wanted to strike, and then there were the guys that said, "Let's blow up the mine." Even though they worked in the mine. It wasn't well thought out but, again, they had that cool brand name. As with Billy the Kid, branding was everything. Branding cattle and branding yourself during these wars. So if you were called the Molly Maguires, you would get a lot more recruits than if you called yourselves the Order of Sincere Coal Miners Looking to Effect Substantive Change.

In those days, people were about the money. If you got in their way, they would try to kill you first. No lawsuits. It created a lot of unique vocations. You couldn't use the army or the police to repress the people because it was bad optics and went against everybody's idea of ourselves as America so, instead, enterprising people came up with their own ways to make money off our inability to confront the flaws in our system. Like . . .

Pinkertons were the first corporate militia. They were legal vigilantes. Pinkerton looked for the craziest, most violent bastards in each community. Somebody who would get off the train in a strange community and just start swinging a club at a guy with soot on his face. Normally that would be illegal, but because they had a business license it was okay. They also, in fairness, went after the Wild Bunch and the James Gang, etc. They stopped some train robberies. But ultimately they were mercenaries and ended up killing for Big Steel and Big Oil and Big Silver, etc. And no one has ever figured out how to make it *fair* for everybody. No system. Democracy came close. But the more money you have, the more money you think you need.

The story of America's civil wars is the story of how society started even as recently as the mid-twentieth century. Before that the strongest survived. Land got claimed by the boldest and the meanest and the most desperate. The political discourse was poisoned wells, attacking trade posts, bushwhackers, horse thieves, highwaymen. And the legal system was gunfighters, posses, "wanted" posters. That's the way every society starts. You have to find people that also got robbed and ask them if they are willing to join with you to set up a system of law. And you can't wait for the government to send troops. And maybe that's why the West still has that attitude about government interference. Because they liked taking the law into their own hands. It's more efficient. And it's probably more satisfying. I mean, as civilized as our system is, how many times are people frustrated when the court lets the killer free? Getting three other townsfolk and riding out to deliver an instant judicial ruling is probably a great feeling. You ride back laughing and when you come into town, the whole town is smiling at you.

That's why in every movie and TV show since they began, the bad guy is either a rich guy or an arm of the government or has an English accent. It's always authority against the little guy. You never see a movie where the little guy is the villain. Unless there's a littler guy that he's abusing. It's got me realizing why the Patrick Swayze classic *Roadhouse* was the greatest modern Western. Because Ben Gazzara was the evil "rancher" in some wide-open western state and Patrick Swayze came to clean up this town. Only instead of shooting up the saloon, Ben Gazzara has his gang drive a monster truck over all the cars at the auto dealership. Every Western you see from *Shane* to *Deadwood,* there's a lot of disturbed people, but there's one evil leader of the damned. The guy who just can't control himself. And they want to be the government. And then the other people eventually band together and kill him. And then hold elections. And that's what America did. We had England as the evil leader. We killed them. And started our own government. But as we spread out, states interpreted law and freedom in different ways.

★ ★ ★

NEVADA

THE SHADOW STATE

It's hard even to talk about Nevada because you know you're just thinking about Las Vegas. Nevada went from being a giant desert to being a giant ashtray. It's all about gambling. The state was just a sandbox waiting for the mafia to come in and give them some ideas. That's what happened. In 1947, Bugsy Siegel looked at the place and realized that, every couple of years, good, God-fearing Americans want to travel someplace where they can go against all their deepest held beliefs, morals, and values. People need a place to be wicked. In Vegas, all bets (as it were) were off: good, honest golden-rule followers who were early to bed, early to rise; chaste; and sober could get drunk, pass out, piss their pants, and have a great weekend. It was the opposite of the way you're supposed to treat your spirit and it's the opposite of the way a body is supposed to be treated. A body is supposed to go to sleep early, plenty of sunlight, no stress, plenty of vegetables, water. In Vegas you go to sleep when the sun comes up, stress all day, and wait in line for carbs, dehydrated and smoking.

That's why Vegas was called Sin City.

The place where you were supposed to cast out your demons. Let off steam. All the deadly sins were there: gluttony (buffet), lust (nude reviews), greed (the tables), envy (tell people you went so they feel jealous), pride (brag how much you won), sloth (sleep all day/party all night), wrath (curse out the dealer when you lose).

Vegas is a great unifier. It's one of the only places where people from different social groups interact. A soccer mom, a cartel drug dealer, an indentured servant from a province in China—all unified. If we ever want world peace, we should set up giant blackjack tables in the UN General Assembly room. It actually looks like a sports book at a casino. The dealers are there to be bonded against. They have to handle people turning on them. They know how temporary love is. When you're winning, you love them. And when you're losing, you hate them. By laying it on the dealer, you don't blame the casino itself. The floor manager and everybody else would sympathize with you. Get you drinks, get you food, a nice room, or tickets to a show. But those goddamn dealers. It's like blaming the bartender for making you drink too much. Unless you are playing the machines. Then it looks like you are alternately cursing at robots and giving them hand jobs.

In the beginning, Vegas was also a place to be elegant. Everybody wore suits and dresses. Because that's how society was. There was one guy whose job it was to slap people around for untucking their shirts at the roulette table. Now people are stumbling around in jorts and Death Cab for Cutie muscle Ts. The rest of the state? Literally nothing has ever occurred there. I'm not exaggerating. Name something. Boulder Dam? That's part of Vegas. The rest of the state you've heard of is just imitation Vegas: anybody for Tahoe, Reno, Laughlin?

There was only one casino town in the whole country. Vegas. It was the trip of a lifetime. When I was growing up, there was an Italian kid I knew in my high school who got sent to Vegas to work because he got in trouble. That was the compromise that the two mob guys must have come up with. He probably robbed something or hit the wrong guy and they said, "Listen, get this kid out of the neighborhood for a couple of years. Send him to Vegas. That kid's going to be a dealer, then become a manager, and then he's going to get involved with the city planning board." He was fifteen, by the way. So Nevada is our first admission that crime pays. It represented that psychological part of the nation that in the 1950s was churchgoing, simple, humble people, but it said, "There's that repressed side." Nevada is the Carl Jung of states.

★ ★ ★

COLORADO

THE EAST OF THE WEST

Colorado is the big shot in its neighborhood. Like New York is the star of the Eastern Seaboard and Massachusetts is the big shot of New England. Colorado is surrounded by low-key states, to put it politely, so it's not too hard to be interesting. But, still, Colorado really made lemons out of lemonade. In the early days, think about it: mountains were just a pain in the ass. Because they were blocking you from getting to the next place. There was no skiing, snowboarding, or bobsledding. The only recreational activity was survival. It was your hobby and your vacation and your relaxation time and your job. But then somebody invented skiing (it doesn't matter who, probably some Norwegian), and next thing you know, a state that was basically a wall that prevented you from getting to California to dig for gold became a fun place to hang out with family and friends. Nature gave Colorado a Disneyland. They didn't have to sign a contract with an entertainment company and then search for people to put on costumes and dance around. People flocked to Colorado because being a ski instructor was a cool and sexy job. Dressing up in a barbershop quartet outfit doesn't have the same allure for some reason. Holding up a *Finding Nemo* puppet in front of a bunch of three-year-olds with ADD who can't shut the fuck up doesn't have the same cachet as a blonde nineteen-year-old conquering one of man's oldest obstacles eight times a day. It took the average prospector three generations to get down that mountain, and these little bastards in Patagonia and stretch pants do it in four minutes. Skiing wasn't popular until 1961, when suddenly every movie had a scene where the master secret agent or the glamorous mystery woman goes to a ski resort in Switzerland. Switzerland was the most popular country from 1961 to 1979. They had all the banks, all the rich people, and all the skiing. And Colorado probably looked at Switzerland and said, "We can be the Switzerland of the United States." And they pulled it off. They made ski resorts out of their mountains and people go there all winter. Now it's true that there's a lot of downtime between May and October. But you can't do anything about the seasons.

Colorado was unique in some ways, but in other ways they did what every state did. They mined whatever metals they had, they planted on whatever soil they had, they got contracts from the feds for the Air Force Academy and to build roads into the Continental Divide to make it easier to get access for their tourist attractions. Every state has to try to figure out how to keep going. What do we have? How can it be turned into a business? And Colorado is lucky because they have a reputation, and reputations, for good or ill, are difficult to break. The skiing is probably better in Utah and Idaho, but Colorado is cooler. They know how to accommodate the needs. You ski in those other states, there's not even a hotel. There's not even a bathroom. You have to take down your ski pants in the middle of a snowy field. I don't know why Colorado became more popular than all the surrounding states in the frontier days. Did the Rockies just make people say, "I'm stopping here"? Or does the Continental Divide have some mystical effect on people where they just say, "Okay, what am I trying to prove? I'm far enough away from my family. Obviously, gold was a big motivator for me but it's also becoming clear that I've been running away from myself."

During the Civil War, the U.S. government granted a lot of places statehood before the Confederates could get their mitts on them, and Colorado was one of those places. You would think that a state based on a rush job for greedy people wouldn't lead to stability, but I guess it shows character is not necessarily a winning ingredient for success. Greed and outside forces and timing can do the job just as well. So, congratulations, Colorado, everybody thinks you're cool, but you and I know you were just in the right place at the right time.

MONTANA

BLANDLANDS

You are the state all the Hollywood stars bought ranches in so they could "get away from it all." Think about that expression. Get away from it all. What is "all"? People, jobs, laughs, excitement. I know you think you are exciting. What about your hiking trails? Nobody has to travel a thousand miles to take a walk and then sit home later with a windburn and twigs in your clothes. What do you talk about in Montana? Nothing. After the second day, what do you discuss? Nothing. Maybe Montana should combine with the other states and form a bigger state. The Balkans did it. Like a state supergroup. Like when Dylan and Tom Petty, etc. formed that mediocre supergroup in the 80s: the Traveling Wilburys. What a disappointment that was. The name alone stinks and their music was tepid. Roy Orbison, who everybody has to worship for whatever reason, and George Harrison, who went from working with John and Paul to having to listen to Bob Dylan tell angry Joan Baez stories all day in his whiny voice. He was doing good on his own, George. But he probably could never sell a ticket. That's like Montana. It's the George

Harrison of states. It's great, but who cares? It can't sell tickets. Because there's overkill, even in nature. Snow is beautiful and deer are beautiful. Too much snow and too many deer are aggravating. It's like too much of anything. Snow is great until you are eleven years old and then it's a pain in the ass until death. Once you retire your sled, it sucks. All those little kids that love snow—I'd like to see how they'd be if they had to drive around in it. That'd change their attitude in a minute. And deer are beautiful from a distance, but up close they give you ticks and eat all the shrubs in your yard. They cause Lyme disease. Deer are lucky they have pretty eyes. It just goes to show you can get away with a lot more bull-shit when you are good-looking. Can you imagine if deer looked like moles? And they gave us Lyme disease? We would have squadrons of Special Forces out there with flamethrowers looking to wipe them out. You would treat deer like the plague bringers they are. But because of their big velvet-brown eyes, everybody loves them. Even I look at a deer and I think, "Mmm . . . I get it." I'm not one of those animal-sex types, but if you have to play F, Marry, Kill with a deer, a mole, and a parrot, you'd probably marry the parrot, so at least you could have a conversa-tion once in a while, kill the mole, and, I hate to say it, F the deer. This is the kind of choice you never have to think about, thank God. Unless you live in an isolated place like Montana. Because it's so quiet there and there's nothing to do, so you end up in these hypothetical decisions like what animals would you F, marry, or kill. So, in the long run, you're talking about a state that people avoided on their way out West for good reason. And those that remained have engaged in questionable practices during those long winter months.

The Louisiana Purchase gave us part of Montana, and the Oregon Treaty gave us the rest. I guess France and England felt like, "We are never going to get over there, so what are we doing? Let's just sell it." Then the United States put up Fort Benton, a military and trading post, on the Missouri River, and it became the hot club to get into. That's what you would do. Put up a trading post and a fort. Then you had the military to protect people but also a trading post so people paid up what they owed the government. One good thing about the show *F Troop* when I was a kid was that it didn't sugarcoat frontier life. It was a popular sitcom that little kids would watch, but it was about a trading post at a fort, and every episode was about corruption, the black market, and stealing among the troops and the local tribes and the traders. It was *Deadwood* for eight-year-olds.

Montana is also famous for the Battle of Little Big Horn (Custer's Last Stand). That was a great victory for the Lakota, the Sioux, the Blackfoot, etc. But it didn't matter. They were doomed. Crazy Horse turned himself in and Sitting Bull hightailed it to Canada. Where he probably got treated like a king for a few years, and then the stories kept repeating, like Bob Dylan's Joan Baez stories, and people started to avoid his teepee. But at least Crazy Horse died as a warrior. You have to figure he got the name Crazy for a reason. Although today it sounds derogatory. Today he'd be called Unresolved Childhood Issues Horse. Montana has a violent past and now it's just the veteran dreaming of the fight, fast asleep at the traffic light. (See Jackson Browne in the Indiana chapter.)

★ ★ ★

IDAHO

THE SLEEPING BAG STATE

Originally incorporated as a parking lot for Utah, Idaho really grew into its own. It's got the beauty of Wyoming combined with the boredom of Iowa. It's not a place you want to be for more than two hours, but in those two hours you'll learn more about how to field dress a deer than you would've thought necessary. TV started in Idaho too. Philo Farnsworth (the guy who came up with television) was born in Idaho. And if there's a more American invention than television, I'd like to hear about it. An outdoor state that invented TV: the ultimate irony! The point is that there's a certain type of person who likes to go into the woods and into the outdoors. The most peaceful and the most violent intermingle in the outdoors. You have beer-drinking hunters and hydrating hikers and sherry-sipping bird watchers. None of those types are on my short list of people to spend time with, by the way. Idaho isn't the kind of place you would think of other than a destination for trout fishing with an estranged brother who thinks waders are Gucci loafers.

Idaho is also known for a canyon that's deeper than the Grand

Canyon—according to them, anyway. I don't know how you'd measure without putting yourself in grave danger. And why would you do it? Just to catch Idaho in a lie? Well, that might be pretty satisfying; I admit it. They are also known for their birds of prey: eagles/falcons/hawks. You wear a straw hat in Idaho and you're asking for trouble. Or a hat that looks like a rodent, I guess. A man like Jim Norton would want to walk cautiously around there. He might get snatched up off the side of a mountain after being mistaken for a baby goat. Watching his flailing legs as he's carted off to become lunch for a family of eagles would probably be visually hilarious, but it's pretty horrible when you think about it. The state motto is *Esto perpetua,* which means "this is forever." Boy, they got that one right. Spend a week in Idaho and you'll feel it. I don't know what they do for money. I guess people love trout—it's always on the menu—but people mostly get salmon. For some reason, salmon gets great publicity, while trout is an afterthought. It's like everybody talks about Bruce Springsteen, but nobody gives any love to John Cougar Mellencamp. Okay, nobody's saying JCM is the boss. But he's got some great Americana tunes, and you don't have to act like he's invisible! But try telling that to the average person who asks the waiter about the trout and who, after he describes it, goes, ". . . I think I'll have the salmon." Okay, whatever. Trout is just the luck of the draw. It's a popularity contest. Trout was the most popular fish in America. Then one day it became all about salmon. And now you never hear about trout. Even writing about it right now is annoying me. But life is a popularity contest. You might be the salmon in your family or you might be the trout. Or you might be the shrimp, whom everybody loves, even though you are a bottom feeder. I don't know you; I don't know your family. I'm staying out of it.

Idaho is where Hemingway killed himself. So that should tell you something. I call him Hemingway instead of Ernest Hemingway so people will think I read all his books—nobody would have the balls to use shorthand unless they did, right, gang? Hemingway is considered *the* great American writer, and he lived through the Spanish Civil War and tragic French love affairs, and heartbreak and betrayal and World War II, and yet it took Idaho to finally make him think, "Life is pointless." That should be Idaho's state motto: "We took Hemingway's spirit."

What will Idaho be if the United States gets divorced? They will go one of two ways: they will either become more withdrawn and stay in their room, or they will try to be the "fun" state to all the other states. Because Idaho is a free spirit. Not a hippie free spirit, like an Oregon or a Vermont, but like your friend who loves to go camping and live in nature. So if the country breaks up, I can see them just saying, "I give up," and then throwing themselves into wilderness. Not a weird mountain man—that would be Wyoming, maybe, or a Dakota—but one of those almost anorexic, compulsive iron-man-contest types who are always training for a triathlon.

Idaho is one of about eight states that will be able to live off the land if things go sour. Maybe they'll form their own country. Them and the big-sky conference. Call them the Big Snore Conference. Or maybe that'll be the Midwest. Call them the United States of Camping. The president can be the CEO of Bass Pro Shops. Go back to frontier justice. They can be a place people come to visit, to breathe air, as in one of those oxygen bars. And if you want fresh water, Idaho can supply it. Why are we drinking all these other waters that were manufactured in Fiji? What's so great about the waters in Fiji? I never heard about them being so great until they became a business. Didn't they just have to pay off a bunch of families of people that died during the hydrogen bomb testing in the 1950s? Are you telling me *that* didn't get in the water? Now you might say, "Didn't they do that in Idaho too?" Yeah but Idaho didn't get sick because they have such good genetics. Because that's why these states were included in the United States. To be the natural beauty states. You know, you always have one kid who's really athletic and healthy? Not interesting but happy? That's Idaho.

So if we break up, Idaho will be just fine. They have the potatoes and the mountains. And that's enough. Give them a backpack and a fishing pole. I salute you, Idaho, as you sit by the campfire and realize that the United States was never really your style, anyway. It always felt a little noisy and busy. You had nothing in common with all these townsfolk. You are happiest hearing a lark sing and getting the fisheye from an owl or getting the owl eye from a fish or putting your ear to the ground, because it doesn't look stupid out there when you do that.

★ ★ ★

WYOMING

THE RAY DAVIES OF STATES

I don't know what to tell you. I tried to stop by recently, and I rang the bell and sat outside, and there was nobody home. Maybe you should rent yourself out for events for the other states. You have a lot of potential in the commercial real estate business. Other than the lack of standing structures, you've certainly got good bones, as they say. Open concept comes to mind. Have you thought about it? You could probably get zoning approval since you haven't started construction yet.

Wyoming has both Grand Teton and Yellowstone, but you can't compare them, because Yellowstone is *famous*. Grand Tetons was just a tit joke on *Married with Children* a few times. Yellowstone has always had a better publicist. But you can't tell them apart: they're like Jesse Eisenberg and Michael Cera. If you meet them, don't panic, just say, "I love your work." I can't say, "I love your work" to a national park, obviously, but I could say it to the park rangers, I guess. I mean they probably will be happy just to hear a human voice. It's one of those jobs where you have to like being alone a lot. Commune with nature, meditate, maybe load and unload your gun. If you're a park ranger, you're basically a state police officer for bears and coyotes. Every other animal, you don't have to even investigate, but those two are capable of crimes of violence, as they've proven numerous times. And wolves. I don't even know if they have wolves up there, but I meant if they do. And raccoons. Because raccoons are not criminal, but they are threatening and like to damage property. Garbage cans. Malicious mischief, I believe they call it.

Cheyenne is the biggest city in Wyoming with 60,000 people—the size of my graduating class in high school, if you count the lunch ladies, which is what most people in Cheyenne probably dress like. Jackson Hole is the "cool" ski resort for people that don't want to be like the douches in Aspen or Park City. They are more of the "down-to-earth douche," the guys who keep reminding you how they're not like those other douches. Then you've got the fact that most of the state are cowboys, which is kind of cool. Riding around the prairie all day on horses. I know today it's probably considered uncool and cowboys are considered an arm of the imperialist genocide of the native peoples (Cowboys and Indians was a game we played when I was young, now the kids probably play Oppressors and First Nations), but I will say this much: for better or worse, cowboys were cool. They had the hats, the horses, the swagger, the growth of beard. Once you are on a horse, you are cool. Any horse. Once they got off the horse, I'm sure a lot of cowboys didn't hold up. I'm sure they disappointed a lot of giggling maidens when they stepped off the horse and they looked like idiots, but a hat and a horse can make you look pretty cool. It's like a nice car and sunglasses. Although cowboys didn't have sunglasses, which is sad: if anybody ever needed them, it was those dudes. Sunglasses weren't invented yet. You had to squint into the sun, and I guarantee that many guys lost duels because they were on the wrong side of the sun.

Then you have Old Faithful. That geyser. That seems like one of those things you need to see when you're there, but you have to force yourself to think about it to be impressed. It's not a natural response. It's more like, "Wow, it's been around for how long? Man, that's insane."

Wyoming also has a lot of mineral extraction. So, on the surface they are not much, but what's going on underneath is pretty powerful. It's like the Kinks. They don't look like rock stars, but when you listen to them, you go, "Wow, that was some real music." Here's something you don't know. The first state to give women the right to vote? Wyoming, in 1869! That blows your mind, right? You don't see them that way. Colorado, Utah, and Idaho are the next three. It's insane, I know. What does it mean? Maybe because they were states that didn't have many people? I know for Wyoming it was probably because they couldn't get any chicks to move there. So the right to vote was probably a kind of a ladies-drink-free type of marketing technique. And it still didn't work. How many women are there in Wyoming? I don't know. Even *they* don't know. Oh well, Wyoming. Your name starts with the question, Why? And doesn't that say it all? Lot of unanswered questions, Wyoming. You're mysterious, the last cowboy, looking over your shoulder as you ride out of town. *Vaya con Dios,* stranger.

UTAH

THE CHURCH OF STATES

The thing with Utah is that they never went for that separation of church and state. I admire them. The rest of the country has been moving away from religion, and Mormons are saying, "We don't give a shit." (I don't know if they curse—probably not—"We don't give a rip.") Utah is a beautiful state. When I went to Salt Lake City, it was just me, and every three blocks is a homeless camp. It's very apocalyptic, but even that's biblical. The only thing I don't like about Mormons and Utah is that they let non-Mormons live there among them. It's weird to have all these people that don't even drink caffeine and then next door, people are drinking and doing meth. They should've made it a dry state. If you have dry counties, why can't you have dry states? It's like opening a strip club in the basement of a church. Even if you aren't looking at them, you know they are downstairs somewhere, and it ruins the service. The priest is talking about spirituality and positivity and you hear the bass line thumping from underneath the floorboards. That's Utah's big mistake. People in the United States like to think of themselves as inclusive and tolerant over all other values. And they are great values, but like anything else they can be taken too far. If you include a street gang in your kids' birthday party, that would be an example of inclusion being bad. Speaking of inclusion, BYU is also known to have a good basketball team, even though it's all white guys. They always have one great white Mormon guard: Jimmer Fredette, Danny Ainge, and Nick Emery, even though he got all their wins vacated for a scandal where a booster gave him a free vacation resort trip and tix to a Broadway show. Even Utah's scandals are PG. Most players on other D1 teams are getting Vegas sex trips and new Porsches, and at BYU they give you a three-day spa treatment and orchestra seats to *Dear Evan Hansen*. The other thing I admire about Mormons is that they go on mission once a year while the rest of the country is going on spring break. Yes, while most kids are doing cannonballs in a molly coma off a balcony in South Padre, these kids are reading the LDS Bible to malaria victims in Sierra Leone.

Utah's state bird is the seagull because seagulls saved the people of Utah from starvation when swarms of crickets threatened to wipe out their crops. The seagulls ate them, I guess. Or else they chased them out and said, "Don't come back." Probably ate them. But it's a reminder about how this country used to be. You had to worry about crickets and boll weevils and locusts and beetles and stink bugs. It's been a constant battle of man vs. bugs since time began. We try to be nice and plant and farm, and these bloodsuckers come in and destroy the whole thing. It makes me angry because we progressed to the point where we invented pesticides that poison them, and then those pesticides end up poisoning us too! It's like how that hunter used to try to kill Bugs Bunny and always ended up blowing himself up. It really makes me sympathize with that idiot, Elmer Fudd, or whatever his name was. I used to be a Bugs Bunny guy, but now that I'm thinking about it, I realize Bugs was a pestilent bastard. Even his first name: Bugs! Same with Woody Woodpecker. And Porky Pig, who often played the hunter and was the bad guy but was actually just trying to survive. You've got to be careful when you get rid of nature. Even plague control can trip you up. For all his faults, Mao Tse-tung had a great idea: the four pests' campaign. Get rid of the big-four disease-ridden, flying, scurrying plagues: rats, flies, mosquitos, and. . . . sparrows? Sparrows apparently ate seeds and fruit. So people started to kill them all over China. They had contests where people would get rewards for bringing in the most rat tails, dead bugs, and dead sparrows. All was well until, the next year, they realized that there was less rice than before and people were starving. Because sparrows didn't just eat seeds, they ate locusts and other pests. Mao Tse-dumb had upset the ecological balance. And so they laid off the sparrows and changed the fourth pest to bedbugs, which was a good idea, but too late. The Great Famine had begun.

Great Salt Lake was first thought to be the Pacific Ocean by the early arrivers, but it's nine times saltier than the ocean. Five billion tons of salt. Remember when salt was considered bad for your health? Now nobody asks how much salt is in anything. Now people are on the warpath against gluten, and the good days for salt are here. Salt can finally say, "We made it through the storm. We were hated for years, and now it's our time to shine. Let gluten take the fall. We are on the right side of history." It just goes to show—you hang around long enough, it comes around to you. Utah has the most charitable people in the country according to amount of volunteer work and percentage of donated income. Well, yeah, if that's how you measure charity, I guess they are. Utah is one of the most mocked states too. Because anybody that's too religious, people make fun of. It's easy and you know they aren't going to fight back. You don't hear a lot of Crips and Bloods humor for that reason. But you hear a lot of Mormon and Christian insults and mockery. Utah is that religious relative that you make fun of, but if they stopped going to church and started hanging out in the bar with you, you'd feel like, *why*? Like John Travolta's brother in *Saturday Night Fever*. It was awkward. So, keep being "U," Utah. We need you, even though it's a little embarrassing to admit it.

THE CORONAVIRUS EPILOGUE

All these western states are looking in the mirror right now, saying, "Yeah, I'm so boring. But now you want to pay attention to me. Now you want social distancing? We have it. That's our number one tourist attraction. You go to the most crowded place in one of our states and there's nobody there. You won't see a person for a week." They have been six feet apart since 1890.

There's not a lot of people, but that's starting to be a plus. Everybody is going to move to the Dakotas, the Idahos, etc. This is what happens every hundred years. The cities empty out and everybody goes back to nature. Then after a generation they realize nature is boring and they move back to the city. So now you will have all these people moving to the country. And twenty years from now, all the big cities will be Billings, Fargo, and Cheyenne. And the hick towns will be New York, Miami, and LA. And the red states will turn blue because all the liberals will move there, and the blue states will turn red because they will all be immigrants who are all about family and religion. And the cities will look like suburbs and the suburbs will look like the country and the country will look like cities.

★ ★ ★

THE PACIFIC
COAST

I don't want parole, I'm too busy working on my website.
—CHARLES MANSON

★ ★ ★

CALIFORNIA

THE AMERICAN DREAM STATE

California is the most important state. By far. Because it's the American dream's American dream. You were the last stop on our whole journey. (Hawaii was us reaching off the bag in many ways, but we'll get to that later.) Back in the old days, people wanted to come out to discover gold. So you got a lot of dirtbags who wanted to get rich. Because if I say there's free money, people are going to bum-rush the place. Look at the Black Friday sales!! Now imagine that, only when you get into Best Buy they have free gold!! I'm sure there were a lot of people who left empty-handed or waited to see who was riding out of California with a smile on his face. That would be the hardest part. Telling your whole crew: "Keep a poker face when we leave." It's like leaving the casino. People ask, "How'd you do?" And you have to shake your head and say, "Not good."

The gold rush got people used to sitting in traffic jams in LA. I remember when I was a kid, Johnny Carson would make jokes about the smog and the freeway all the time. Now everybody has freeway traffic, but back then it was only LA. Now it's a given in Southern California that if you have to be at work at 8 A.M., you have to leave as soon as you pull into your driveway the night before.

Johnny Carson gave us all the information about California every night. He made jokes about the "fruits and nuts" (double entendres about gays and health food). And plastic surgery. And drugs. And all the cults and therapies and group sex and hippies, and he basically spread the culture of California to the the rest of us. He had the ear of the entire country. Nobody was more powerful from 1965 to 1985 than Johnny Carson. He probably had people killed. I'm sure people tried to blackmail him (wouldn't you?), and I'm sure he just talked to his producer, Freddie de Cordova, and he'd take care of it. That's how powerful *The Tonight Show* was. Everybody knew the *producer's* name and personality. It was a lot of power, and Johnny just sat back and smiled and drank and smoked and fucked and played tennis and just made sure he was in Burbank every afternoon to crack jokes about the fairies on Santa Monica Boulevard and Governor Reagan and all other things California.

California was the place that only the gay family member or the hot girl was allowed to move to, to try and get famous. The pretty ones went to LA, the smart ones went to New York—that's the way it's always been. California was what the hometown people could wrap their heads around. You would never have caught nerds in Hollywood either, until they started financing the films. Nerd taste has taken over the industry. Every actor in Hollywood is wearing a Halloween costume and carrying a shield. Martin Scorsese said it best—"You nerds aren't making movies"—and he's no alpha male himself. He's a half nerd, what we call a street nerd.

But the weirdest thing about California is still that accent. That valley girl/surfer accent that is somehow not as annoying as it should be. There's something about it that kind of grows on you. It's like they're always talking from a chaise lounge on the beach or something. It's sunny in California, and they never get overly emotional. It's where they invented "dude" and "bro." "Dude" is an all-encompassing word: it's a way of being casual but can mean "best friend" or "the clerk behind the counter" or "sister" or "brother." And to Californians, "bro" works the same way, which is pretty impressive.

But I've been worried about you, California. Because you have all those fires every year that destroy property and take lives and cost billions. With much beauty comes much disaster. Like you date a hot girl, you have to deal with the psycho ex-boyfriend and her Xanax addiction and her screaming-crying drama whenever you go out in public. Your fires are like that. And then all those brave volunteer firemen have to put their lives at risk to put them out. And every year you ask the volunteer firemen to come fight the fires, and they do it. I want to ask you something. Have you ever thought, "These fires happen every year; we should probably hire some permanent fireman instead of being surprised every year and relying on volunteers?" Maybe the cliché that you people are a little bit brain-dead is actually true.

Then you have the water shortage. Everybody thought it was gonna be air that went first. Isn't that just like life? Your doctor tells you he wants to talk about your X-ray, and you get hit by a car walking over to his office. Meanwhile, help is right upstairs and they won't answer the door!! Seattle has enough water for everybody. Record rainfalls! How hard would it be to run a pipeline down to their neighbor? But they're not going to. They're going to let you be dehydrated. Because that's the thing about being beautiful and fun. People love you but they envy you, and when you start to fall apart, they enjoy it. Oh yeah, everybody loved Southern California in the 70s and 80s. But not so much now that you're dry-lipped with a parched throat. In ten years, you'll look like the walking dead.

LA, you are really where the American dream ended. The beach, the yachts, the mansions, the sex, the glamour. LA would let people know they had their number: "You know why you came out here. Stop bullshitting. You want a safe life in a cubicle? Don't bother coming out." You guys ran shit. You guys were the no-apologies dream factory. Now you make movies about a bunch of comic book superheroes and cartoons, because that's what the nerds in cyberspace tell you they want. *You* used to tell people what *they* wanted. What happened? Every movie had a mansion in the background or was set on the beach. There were no dystopian-landscape movies shot in LA. LA was only for the homecoming. It was the victory lap of the movie after you killed the bad guys. Then they'd show a house in Tujunga, and everybody in the world would go, "Yeah, that's where I want to live." Seeing the Sunset Strip was on everybody's bucket list. And then a couple of nerds found a way for everybody on the planet to have their own network and it was over. That's the internet.

The power dynamic of modern culture shifted when Northern California caught Southern California slipping. While SoCal was busy doing coke and going to awards shows, the nerds up north took over the state on their way to taking over the planet. Just because the nerds were ugly, you kicked them to the curb, and next thing you know it's payback time. You used to be cocky, and now they're cocky. Power corrupted Northern California the way Communism corrupted Russia. You had the quiet, chubby farmer in Odessa: once they put him in charge of rationing potatoes, he became Harvey Weinstein. Like Silicon Valley back in the 90s. The nerds were suddenly the kings of the valley. They spent the 70s getting slapped around their towns and the 80s being computer geeks, and by the 90s they were the equivalent of football heroes. Hipsters came out of that. Hipsters were nerds rebelling against nerds. SoCal, Northern California took over your business and gave it out for free on YouTube!!

And now you've lost your identity. You were the beautiful dummies. And now you are trying too hard to be intelligent. You are trying to be like the NoCal nerds. It's not you. Did you watch the Sunday-morning political shows until ten years ago? Of course not. You were at a pool party for eighty years. Now you are tweeting all day in your house like a shut-in psycho from Michigan. Looking up local election coverage and watching MSNBC with the curtains closed. You are rich, but you can't even enjoy it. You are caught between your conscience and your true nature. You are living in the land of milk and honey, but you have to act like you are in a Soviet farming collective. You can't wear makeup because of the harm testing it does on animals, you can't dress too attractively because it's objectifying, you can't drive an expensive car because of the environment, and you can't make funny comedy movies or TV shows because the funny ones don't have the right message.

NoCal really threw you off your game. You used to tell them what to do. You would go up to NoCal to get drunk in Napa Valley and then fly back the same night. Now you have to go up there hat in hand and beg for money from a guy who invented an app that lets you have sex with strangers within walking distance of the best frozen yogurt place. They put the dream factory in everybody's hand, and now in Norma Desmond's closeup she's in a superhero mask.

You used to be the nation's voice. And that voice was fun, even though you still got to feel like you were delivering important messages. Now it's like getting lectured by a traveling monk during the Inquisition. Everything is atonement for past sins and self-flagellation. You're still taking the money and the houses, only you feel like you shouldn't be so showy about it. But you are still making sure you travel and send your kids to wherever they want to go to school and getting internships, and that's all natural. But you can't do that and then scold other people who do it too. Unless you actually take vows of poverty and give up all your worldly possessions, you are just like those old popes selling indulgences so people feel better about themselves while you live the good life. And then a Savonarola or a Martin Luther comes along and takes you down. Nailed the 95 Theses on the door of Wittenberg Castle. Which is kind of annoying, like anybody is going to read 95 things. It's so close to 100—you could've put 5 more in there. Just to make it more dramatic. Nobody would read them all, but nobody read all 95 anyway.

But the point is: California did it right!! They had it and they went all the way with it. And when it's over, it's over.

★ ★ ★

OREGON

WE WERE A STATE BEFORE IT WAS COOL

Oregon is the kid in school that always has to be different. If everybody wants to play football, they're the kid that starts a shuffleboard team. Oregon was always its own, unique self. It's the only state in the United States that had people killed in World War II on its soil. A Japanese balloon bomb killed six people in Oregon. The Japanese sent over a bunch of hot air balloons and over three hundred of them landed in America! But most were discovered and detonated, except for the one in Oregon in 1945.

Lewis and Clark started the Oregon Trail, and the state is named after it, even though it ran through Washington, Idaho, and Oregon. The other two decided to rebrand, I guess. Oregon was an equal partner to Washington as fellow losers for most of their lives and then suddenly . . . Microsoft! Boom! Starbucks! And suddenly Oregon is the poor neighbor. I've had it happen to me in comedy, when somebody I came up with and was parallel to becomes really famous and . . . I get it's not a good feeling.

And Oregon was the original!! They were hipster even before Washington was. They've always been into organic food; and, yes, the Nike store was a big thing; and the Trailblazers and nature and food co-ops and bike rights and veganism and anticorporate riots. They had Antifa in the 1820s, protesting corporate takeover of the beaver-pelt industry. They were homeless-chic before anybody else. Oregon is very liberal—it's always either the West Coast or the East Coast that's liberal, and the middle of the country is conservative. I wonder how that happened. Maybe the Puritans living on the East Coast from England were more the progressive types as opposed to the Scots, who settled down south. And the systems of law reflected that. Then the Midwest and West practiced frontier law—self-reliance, where you had to be your own police force, doctor. But the West Coast went for a different set of laws. Maybe because they realized they were hitting the wall at the end of the country, or maybe it was because they had the ocean as their front yard so they were more chill. I'm not sure. But you do wonder how much of an effect the early days have on a state's personality later on. Just like a kid. You wonder how much of the family and how much of their early childhood experiences make them who they are. I've always thought this country could use some group therapy sessions, which is really what the Constitutional Convention was.

Because the Oregon Trail went through half the country, it picked up everybody's values and personalities and dumped them out at the end. People could sift through the pile and reinvent themselves and customize their personalities. So, in Oregon you have vegan loggers. You have gun-owning progressives. You combine the values of the whole country into one package—Oregon, the collective individual.

★ ★ ★

WASHINGTON

REVENGE OF THE NERDS

There's something about being at the end of the country. It's got to feel good to know that you are the last of it. Until Hawaii and Alaska kind of stole the thunder. But the fact that we ended up trading Vancouver for you has to feel good, no? 54-40 or fight. That was the line between Canada and Alaska, which Russia owned. But we didn't want to fight, obviously, since we compromised and we took you. Our special little package!

You were known for logging back in the day. Guess what? Nobody needs logs from you. We *all* have trees. But everybody needs to feel useful, so we let you be "that guy" for a number of years. But now that you have Bill Gates and Microsoft, you don't really need to be the tree guy, so the right thing to do would be to hand it off to Montana or even Oregon. Greed is not the answer, you natural resource hoarders.

Bill Gates revolutionized the world. And then he sat back like the world's most famous nerd that he is and then Steve Jobs, who knew less about computers than I do, came in and blew his place up. Talk about being caught slipping! BG was strutting around like a rajah with Microsoft and then this ubersalesman/world's worst boss/sociopath comes along and blows him right off his mountain. Gates got outnerded, and he didn't like it. Because Steve Jobs sold out the nerds and brought down the destruction of mankind by giving non-nerds computer skills. We should not all know how to use computers. When Bill Gates ran things, you had to go to computer school for four years. Now everybody can go into a store and come out with the powers of a programmer from the 90s. It's unnatural. That would be like if we could all walk in and get pilot licenses right now and just start flying helicopters in the sky without skills or training. Crashes, accidents, mayhem. That's what social media is. It's a sky full of untrained, out-of-control helicopters.

Washington is also known for rainfall. That's nothing to be proud of. You didn't do anything. You just are there and it rains and then you act like it's Disneyland. You know, "come up and see our rain." No thanks. It's not a sign of a very entertaining place if the weather conditions are part of your tourism brochure. "We have the best umbrellas and boots." "Shut up! I'll stay put here and wait for June. How's that?" Same thing when you say you are proud of your beautiful mountain ranges. You have nothing to be proud of! They were there when you got there. And when you say, "We are outdoors people. We're all about hiking and climbing." Hey, first of all, those are activities for little babies. Second, how can you do that and still smoke a pack of organic cigs every day??

Washington is also where hipsters were actually invented. That's pretty cool. It started in the late eighties, when everybody in Seattle was reading paperbacks and smoking cloves, and suddenly we had Kurt Cobain and Eddie Vedder and PJ Harvey types—I know she's not from there, but you know what I mean, and don't give me a hard time about it; I'm not in the mood. If you look at the average hipster outfit today—plaid shirt, baggy pants, and beard, etc.—it's how Seattle has been dressing, out of necessity, since about 1850. So that's kind of a thing, I guess. But also, I remember when I was on MTV (yes, I still start sentences like this), we all met these guys at some party, and I remember it was the changing of the guard because everybody was all over these grunge guys and making fun of the hair bands. Which was a little bit disloyal, because they had been the MTV mainstays from the beginning in 1987 to 1991, but that's how it goes in life—when your time is up, people have to insult you to work themselves into a lather so they can feel okay about themselves when they take you down.

I like Washington State, but there's something about them that's not very West Coast. Maybe because Washington is too close to Canada if you consider Vancouver to be Canada, which most good people don't. It's almost like they are trying to be too mournful all the time and they are just too introspective. Guess what? People go out to the West Coast to relax. And it's your responsibility to make everybody able to just let go of their troubles and party and dance. If you want to be depressed, you can move to Delaware or someplace. They will give you something to be depressed about. So just sit there in your ratty sweater and read your Bukowski and stop giving me sullen glances. Be lucky we don't pull your hipster card now that you traded skinny jeans for Dockers and heroin for beta-blockers.

★ ★ ★

THE COUNTRY'S FOSTER CHILDREN

★ ★ ★

ALASKA

THE BAD KIDS

How about the fact that we bought it from Russia in 1867 and Canada didn't even get in on the deal when we basically had to step-walk through their entire country to claim it. And even then, we didn't make Alaska a state till 1959. Because it's such a disturbing place. It's always been home to the parole violators, bail jumpers, fugitives, embezzlers, absconders. All the people in the Lower 48 who wanted to get away from law enforcement, their families, their responsibilities, themselves. They would go up to Alaska, and it was just accepted that if you were desperate enough to go up there, nobody would pursue you. If you wanted to live by yourself and never see any other people, Alaska was the place to do it. But the question is, what kind of people want that? I will tell you. Psychos, loners, people who like to bundle up and cover up their faces most of the time. Nowadays it's a little better, I guess, because you've got the kids that grew up there and are more normal. In some parts of Alaska, they have sixty-day nights. Then they have eighty days of sunlight. Owning a nightclub up there is a pretty sweet move. You never have to close. Then again, eighty days of sunlight with no night sounds good on paper, but it's probably very aggravating. Like everybody's on a meth run. Russia sold Alaska to us in 1867 for two cents an acre. Which seems cheap, but at the time, what were they going to do with a snow-filled darkened room? There's no record of it, but they probably sold it that cheaply because America said, "Meet us in Barrow, the town up north, while it was never light," and then Russia was like, "We have to get rid of this lemon." They didn't realize it wasn't like that in the whole state or even in Barrow all the time. It's an old real estate trick: let a building get run-down so you can buy it cheap. Alaska is an odd place. The clichés are still true. Dog sledding is the state sport, which is probably a little odd. Instead of football heroes, everybody is cheering over some fat kid in a parka who's cursing at huskies.

Being a trapper is an actual job. It's not a hobby. There are guys walking around with wood boxes that can chop your hand off. Every time you take a walk, you have to be careful that you aren't going to end up upside down with one of your feet tied to a tree limb. The smart move Alaska made is that you can't leave Juneau, the capital city. There are no roads out. You are stuck there. So it gives you a little time to think about whatever behavior you're up to. I think we should do that to all the cities. Put up barbed wire around every city, and I bet people will act a lot better knowing they can't just flee. It sounds a little counterintuitive, but it's the right move: instead of keeping people out, keep 'em in. Juneau can be a little scary. Because they have one bear for every twenty-one people. I don't know about you, but I don't like those odds. Alaska should keep to its roots. Anybody that messed up in life should have to live up there for five years. It could be like the therapist state. They could charge people to stay up there like a long-term rehab. And the other citizens would be the counselors. Alaskans can forgive, because they understand that, even if they are normal, their parents and grandparents were the black sheep of the family.

HAWAII

THE JINX

It's one of four states—along with Vermont, Texas, and California—that was an independent nation before it became one of our happy fifty. Hawaii was a monarchy run by kings until they had election riots that let Britain and the United States send troops in. It is one of those things that has happened a lot in history. Troops come in and stop the bloodshed, and then while they are in charge, the countries they represent send in ambassadors and lawyers and businessmen who rewrite the laws so they're unfavorable to the people from the country who already live there. And that's Hawaii. The provisional government overthrows whoever's giving them trouble and then takes over.

Symbolically, it's built on a volcano or something. Hawaii is one of those states that really doesn't want to be here. They were brought in by force/trickery, but they had to know somebody was going to grab them and it was either us or Japan. Japan thinks they own Hawaii, but we are geographically closer to them, so they're our family and we love them. And we have a giant military presence there to remind them of that.

Hawaii was run by powerful sugar-plantation owners until the 1950s, when the descendants voted them out. Hawaii was never meant to be a state. It's got such a fun vibe. Hawaii should just be itself. A fun party place and vacation paradise. Run by an event planner instead of a governor. Somebody who just tells you who's coming that week and what the menu looks like. Sort of a cruise director/governor. Every state should be able to play to its strengths instead of everyone having to fall in line with protecting natural resources, creating jobs and industry, etc. Hawaii doesn't feel like people should even have to work indoors. We should let Hawaii go. They don't like being a state; they are unhappy. Let them be an island nation. But they have to let us have one of the islands on our way out. Maybe the big island. Just give us one for old times' sake and we'll call it a wash.

To add insult to injury when it comes to being part of the United States, Hawaii took the hit for Pearl Harbor, an attack that probably would've hit the naval bases in California otherwise, and it wasn't even a state. But we bonded a little bit after that, or at least I like to think so. The big Hawaiian industries are pineapples, military, tourism, and whaling. But once pot is totally legalized, Hawaii will have the best pot. Like France with wines or Idaho with potatoes. It will be their thing.

Hawaii is embarrassing because it reminds us how we can get too full of ourselves and pull some illegally shady shit when we want something. And we did it in the 1950s because America in the 1950s ruled the world. We were hot off World War II and we were the heroes and we had dropped nukes and we had a great economy and we were helping Europe rebuild, so we were pretty cocky. And we literally went thousands of miles off our country's border and grabbed Hawaii and said, "You are going to be a state." So now we have a state that feels like it has got one foot in and one foot out. It shouldn't be a five-hour plane ride to the next nearest state! But that's how we were in 1959. We would've turned any place we found into a state because we couldn't imagine people not wanting to be with us. We were full of ourselves after World War II. It happens to a lot of countries—and teams, after a couple of Super Bowls. You get cocky. It was right before Vietnam and the protests and riots of the 60s. In 1959 if you said anything bad about America, people all over the world would look at you like you were crazy. And it all started to come apart at the seams in the 60s. Now that I come to think of it, I think Hawaii and Alaska jinxed us! "Aloha" means "hello" and "goodbye." We thought we were saying hello, but maybe we were actually saying goodbye.

THE AMERICAN ROME

The City of Magnificent Intentions.
—CHARLES DICKENS

WASHINGTON, D.C.

THE NATION'S SMOKE-FILLED BACK ROOM

It was the city they chose as the capital when they realized the South was going to leave if they didn't compromise. That was the pivotal move. New York City was the capital—even Philly was the capital for a while, frighteningly enough—and then they let George Washington pick the location, which was donated by Virginia and Maryland. D.C. was obviously built for deals.

It's the place where everybody can put the blame. "Those idiots in Washington," "All that hot air in Washington," hardy har har. It's where everybody tries to make deals for the rest of the country. You've got lobbying firms, industry trade groups, law firms, civilian contractors. And they all have different names and work for different companies, but they all have the same job. To get a lunch or a dinner with a few congressmen or a senator and get them to support whatever bill will help save their industry some money. And so D.C. is really a city built on people trying to redirect some of the power of elected people to their industries. In the old days, it operated by buying the elected officials a few drinks and blackmailing them. I don't know how it's done nowadays. Probably a lot subtler. Maybe helping their kids get into a college or something. I guess a good lobbyist just figures out what an elected official wants and then helps them get it. They sit down, and if they notice you checking out the waiter or waitress, they know you want sex. And if they see you looking at their jewelry or shoes, they know you like clothes and material things. And if you talk about how you hate your house, they know you want to move. But D.C. is *supposed* to be that kind of place. Everybody talks about taking money out of politics, and now maybe they finally can because there are digital fingerprints and footprints. It's like college-sports recruitment. You can't say it out loud—you just have to find ways to lease the tight end's mother an SUV and get the high school coach an assistant job at a major school. Only in Washington, D.C., instead of the mom getting an SUV, it's a congressman's kid on the crew team next to Felicity Huffman's kid. And instead of the coach, it's the congressman's district's largest employer getting a contract. It's corruption, but it's almost natural corruption. We spend a lot of our time trying to root out corruption, but what is corruption? Illegal favors. What are favors? Favoritism. We set up a country where there is no legal favoritism. But favoritism is still going to happen. So maybe the problem is pretending it's not going to happen when it is. Maybe every congressman should get three strikes, you're out. Three under-the-table deals, and if you get greedy, then you lose out. Because you are there to help your district. And if you don't, then everybody hates you and you don't win your next election. And if you bring back jobs, everybody loves you. And where do you get jobs from? Companies that want favors! It's a no-win situation. D.C. is not a state because it's the back room of our country. But nobody wants to admit it. And if people don't want the place to be corrupt, get rid of D.C. being the headquarters of government. Have the federal government be in a different state every year. Travel around. Do it by lottery. One year it's in Michigan, the next it's in Utah. This way everybody gets a chance to have the capital be near them. And everybody in the capital gets to live in the whole country.

> *Americans are not a perfect people, but we are called*
> *to a perfect mission.*
> —ANDREW JACKSON (NOT A PERFECT PERSON)

INVENTORY
OR AUTOPSY?

★ ★ ★

WHEN IN THE COURSE OF HUMAN EVENTS YOU BECOME A NATION OF MALCONTENTS

We set our standards too high. We shot off our mouths and told the world we could save everybody. The Constitution was a big-shot document. This country was supposed to live fast, die young, and leave a good-looking corpse. We weren't meant to be hanging on forever. We set unrealistic goals, "We are going to be the land of opportunity *for everybody. We'll have equality, liberty, justice, happiness.* We know everybody says that, but . . ." The founding fathers should have just said, *"We are starting a country. It's kind of a pop-up. We don't really know how long it will last; we'll see how it goes."* Instead, we jinxed ourselves. We overreached. And we became an empire, and in all empires, you eventually kill each other with infighting.

And then Trump came along and the media freaked out because they didn't realize that, even though he was a psycho, he was a breath of fresh air to people that have been removed from the national dialogue. And he didn't bother them, because most of them work in jobs where the bosses are all like him. So, what, he says racist remarks? So does their boss. So, what, he says grab 'em by the pussy? So does their boss. He doesn't insult the red states and tell them they are thinking, voting, and eating bad. He compliments them and he eats like them. Hardee's. Golden Corral. He doesn't drink smoothies, his smoothie is a cake batter shake from Baskin Robbins. Trump is just the canary in the coal mine, and I don't say that just 'cause they both have the same color hair.

We need a new infrastructure and we have to divide up the place. We take down bridges and put Sheetrock dividers in the roads. All the monuments will get divided during the divorce. Blue states get the Liberty Bell, and red states get Mount Rushmore. All the other national landmarks? Who gets Plymouth Rock? South of the Border? How do we divide up the mountain ranges? This country is on the verge of a civil war and we can't afford it because it'll never stop, it'll go on forever. Because who's going to break it up ? Canada? Mexico? Nova Scotia?

But however this country turns out, nobody can deny that we went for it! It worked as well as anybody else who tried an operation of this magnitude.

People in denial say, "Why can't we be like Denmark?" Because we have nothing in common with Denmark! Denmark is a local grocery store. America is Walmart. In a mom-and-pop, you have maybe six employees and they're all cousins. At Walmart, you have three hundred employees, and if you work in the Patio and Garden, you might never meet the Pharmacy people. And when you do sit next to them in the break room, you have nothing to say. So everybody ends up sitting with their own section, even though they don't necessarily like them.

America has a personality. Everybody does. England's personality was elegant and intelligent from centuries of literature and education. France's personality was seductive from hundreds of years of valuing effortless charisma and style. Japan grew Zen from thousands of years of repetition and ritual and focus. And America was cocky, but in a good way. We were innocent and idealistic, and it was annoying but also refreshing in a world where everybody had become jaded. Americans were workers. Now we are salesmen. And then, like anyone else, our success led us to become obsessed with leisure activities. The world knows us for entertainment: action movies, sports, pop music. All superficial. We are fun. But fun isn't character. Character is in the ghosts of all the soldiers and hookers and farmers that still haunt our roads and trails. The people that would walk through snow in bare feet and then ask a mountain lion, "What are you lookin' at?" Those people are buried in the earth under gyms and car dealerships and dollar stores and in national parks and on the sides of mountains and under stadiums where the teams are named after their ancestors' biggest enemies: wolves, bears, and avalanches.

Those wild people that just said, "Screw everything—I don't need to be near medicine, or stores, or people I can trust; I would rather gamble on death than keep living where I'm living." Their energy made us into a functional country of 50 states.

It was hard to put together this country. We had to replicate our form of government and also put together: Trails. Traders. Treaties. Canals. Railroads. That's what made America's personality. Power Walking. Trading. Negotiating. Digging. Hammering. All these geographic and psychologically diverse places. And the federal government was the operations manager, and everybody always hates their manager.

And the federal system was an attempt to combine the freedom of small states with the growth of large states. And to mitigate power. Everything was about the mitigation of power. There was either too much power in the hands of the electoral or too much in the legislature. We need the tension between state and federal. It's the same with individuals: you need to be able to think for yourselves sometimes, and you need to be part of the collective at the same time.

That's why the Constitution is considered genius. Not because it's so brilliant, but because it's an actual plan. And most things aren't plans. They are just thoughts about what's wrong. And the whole theme of the Constitution was compromise. On paper and in the room. And they made a lot of mistakes. And that's how the country was founded—on people making mistakes. But the power now is not with the people who actually try to do things. It's with the critics. The second-guessers. The Monday-morning quarterbacks. It's a Greek chorus. Life is being lived and narrated by everyone else simultaneously. And we live at a time when smart people will never speak honestly. Because they can lose their job, etc., based on 25 people taking them down on Twitter. So only stupid people tell the truth. Smart people just shut up or say something that panders to everyone in the power circles of media, entertainment, news, and mostly the mob. People speak in empty platitudes that mimic intelligence but mean nothing.

We did what any other country would've done in our circumstances. With that much land and that much potential, we reached for the stars. And we fell short. But we tried. And we were hypocrites, but who isn't? And we were cocky the way anybody would've been. And we were also friendly and welcoming and generous many times. It hasn't been a relentless onslaught of racism and sexism and xenophobia. And it hasn't been an unbiased, colorblind utopia either. It's been a bumpy ride, where sometimes you are amazed at how happy you feel and sometimes you are throwing up out the window. Sometimes you are looking at the scenery and singing along with the radio, and sometimes you are arguing and planning to punch the person driving at the next rest stop.

We did something nobody did before. We let everybody have a personality. We got rid of the idea of the masses and replaced them with individuals. If you thought you were funny, society never tried to stop you from telling jokes. If you thought you were smart, society didn't try to stop you from forcing people to endure your thoughts on everything. The downside is that most people don't know when to shut up. But the upside is that you don't have to listen to the same seven members of the Tudors for five hundred years.

I don't think anybody else came close to finding a way to stay together for this long. And hopefully we will be able to find a way to compromise and go forward. Maybe you have forty states that are pro-choice and ten states that aren't. Forty states that are pro-gun and ten states where you get life in prison for possession of a gun. Maybe we try that with a bunch of laws and see which ones turn out best. And if the country has to break up even after that, then we walk away with dignity. And whatever happens, we can always say, "We used to be America."

> *All the armies of Europe and Asia . . . could not by force take a drink from the Ohio River or make a track on the Blue Ridge in the trial of a thousand years. No, if destruction be our lot, we must ourselves be its author and finisher. As a nation of free men, we will live forever or die by suicide.*
> —Abraham Lincoln

ACKNOWLEDGMENTS

Special thanks to Elizabeth Beier for her insightful notes and Texas attitude. James Fauvell, for his low-key brilliance; it couldn't have happened without you. Brian Stern, for still being excited when we do these things. Andrew Bloom, you will be missed!! Phil Hanley, it took a Canadian to name an American book. To Mike Berkowitz, Eve Atterman, and Marcus Levy, for putting it all together. Larry Shire and Gil Karson and Grubman Indursky. Lia Sweet, for all these years, and Diane Sweeney and everybody at RZO. And my wife, Jen, for putting up with a house full of notes in every nook and cranny. Love you.